Volume 12

THE RUSSIAN WORKERS' REPUBLIC

THE RUSSIAN WORKERS' REPUBLIC

HENRY NOEL BRAILSFORD

Routledge
Taylor & Francis Group

LONDON AND NEW YORK

First published in 1921 by George Allen & Unwin Ltd

This edition first published in 2024
by Routledge
4 Park Square, Milton Park, Abingdon, Oxon OX14 4RN

and by Routledge
605 Third Avenue, New York, NY 10158

Routledge is an imprint of the Taylor & Francis Group, an informa business

© 1921 George Allen & Unwin Ltd

British Library Cataloguing in Publication Data
A catalogue record for this book is available from the British Library

ISBN: 978-1-032-67165-9 (Set)
ISBN: 978-1-032-67297-7 (Volume 12) (hbk)
ISBN: 978-1-032-73136-0 (Volume 12) (pbk)
ISBN: 978-1-003-42687-5 (Volume 12) (ebk)

DOI: 10.4324/9781003426875

Publisher's Note
The publisher has gone to great lengths to ensure the quality of this reprint but points out that some imperfections in the original copies may be apparent.

Disclaimer
The publisher has made every effort to trace copyright holders and would welcome correspondence from those they have been unable to trace.

THE RUSSIAN
WORKERS' REPUBLIC

BY

HENRY NOEL BRAILSFORD

LONDON: GEORGE ALLEN & UNWIN LTD.
RUSKIN HOUSE, 40 MUSEUM STREET, W.C. 1

First published in 1921

PREFACE

THIS book is the fruit of two months spent in the autumn of 1920 in Soviet Russia. A visit to Russia is no longer a difficult adventure. I obtained a British passport to Esthonia and a Russian permit quite easily. Travelling was uneventful, and less uncomfortable than I had found it in Poland, Austria and Germany the year before. I met invariably with kindness and courtesy, and made many acquaintances, who represented every phase of opinion. "White" exiles in London had told me that I should be watched, followed and "personally conducted" wherever I went, and that no opponent of the Communists would dare to talk with me or approach me. None of these predictions came true. I went about *alone* whenever and wherever I wished. I saw the leaders of the opposition *alone* in Moscow. In the provinces the local leaders of the opposition sought me out. Even in trains and libraries, strangers would enter into conversation and express themselves quite freely. Let me say at once that while I heard much criticism in Russia, I never heard there the wild exaggerations in which exiles indulge abroad. So far from receiving too much help from official quarters in my inquiries, I could sometimes have wished for more. There is much kindness but very little method in the dealings of the Bolsheviks with foreign journalists.

I divided my time between Petrograd, Moscow, Minsk and the Western war-front and the central province of Vladímir. Moscow is still incorrigibly Russian, which means that it is unpunctual and unbusinesslike. The distances are great and the communications primitive. The telephone works badly and is little used. The Press reflects only one point of view. One may spend a week in Moscow and learn less than one could gather in two days in Berlin. Everyone, moreover, is overworked, and officials, after the Congress of the Third International, were rather tired, I suspect, of foreigners. In any event, I was anxious to see something of the provinces and of country life. I chose Vladímir for a short visit, and found it so interesting that I remained for two weeks. I learned in these two weeks more about Russia than in the other six. To investigate the life of a small town is a manageable problem. You can walk all over it without fatigue. Also, I could get conveyances to visit the villages, a thing I only once achieved from Moscow. Above all, everyone was interested in the presence of a stranger. Vladímir had seen no foreigner of any sort for six long years, and it was as eager to question me as I was to study it. This mutual inclination led to a stimulating exchange of thought and information. My reasons for choosing Vladímir were partly that it combined industry with agriculture, and partly that it had escaped the ravages of the civil war. I wanted to see the normal development of Soviet institutions after three years of revolution.

My slight acquaintance with the very difficult Russian language was a handicap which I must confess. I had spent some months before I started in an effort to learn it. I could understand a great deal that was said, and could latterly follow a speech, if the orator did not speak too fast. But one easily grows tired in these efforts, and I never managed to express my own thoughts, except in the most elementary way. I can read a newspaper, though with much labour. I had at Vladímir as an interpreter a young man, Comrade Rozinsky, of whose character and ability I formed a high opinion, and he had a tact rare in interpreters : he always left me alone when I did not need his services. Even in remote Vladímir I found a good many people who could talk French, German or English. In Petrograd and Moscow, of course, nearly every educated man, and many a workman who has lived abroad, speaks one of these languages, and usually well. Of the three, I found German the most generally useful. Oddly enough, the Russian of the peasants, which is very pure in the Central Provinces, was easier to understand than that of the intellectuals.

To my friend Michael Farbman, who was in Minsk and Moscow during my stay, I owe many helpful suggestions and explanations, and he has done me the service of reading my proofs—not always with assent.

I have never, in what is now a rather long experience, found an inquiry so difficult. I have never felt so little confidence in my own conclusions. Perhaps I may also add that I have never been more anxious to arrive at the objective truth.

H. N. BRAILSFORD.

Christmas 1920.

CONTENTS

CONTENTS

The Russian Workers' Republic

CHAPTER I

THE FACTORY IN THE FOREST

EVERY whitewashed wall in every Russian town repeats the watchwords of the proletarian Revolution in phrase and picture, in satire and command. It was not from these symbols, nor yet from the bountiful literature of propaganda, that its aim and meaning came home to me most directly. I felt it most clearly of all in a factory amid the forests of Central Russia. A long, straight cobbled road, rough and dilapidated, like everything else in this primitive land, had led us twenty miles out of the provincial capital of Vladímir, an ancient little town, more venerable than Moscow itself, the very heart and centre of the old Great Russia.

We had passed two or three villages, some patches of cultivation, a bare heath and a peat-bog, but they seemed mere clearings in the everlasting forest. On the edge of this forest, near the Moscow–Nizhni-Novgorod railway, a vast cotton factory had been built. Through its endless spinning and weaving sheds a man might walk, as the workmen said, " for versts." It held before the Revolution a population of 12,000 employees, with their numerous children. Never have I seen a place which seemed to enjoy so few obvious advantages for its purpose. A Lancashire cotton-mill stands near to its coal-pit, not very far from the wharves to which its bales are shipped, in a damp atmosphere favourable to spinning. Here, over the sandy soil, the air was brilliantly dry. The oil fuel must come from Baku, a thousand miles away; the coal from the Donetz, about five hundred miles distant; the cotton from Turkestan, a good two thousand miles overland. There was, to be sure, a river, deep and not too swift, which should have been navigable, but it was bridged by floating wooden causeways which no barge could pass.

Ask why it was that capital had fixed on this strange site, and there is only one possible answer. The sandy soil is poor. The cultivation is incredibly backward and primitive. The peasants, illiterate, conservative and prolific, could barely feed themselves from their narrow patches of ill-tilled moorland. The cheapness and abundance of their labour was the one attraction which had drawn capital to this place. No trade union was tolerated here before the Revolution. Every form of association among the workers, even for purposes of education or recreation, was forbidden. I saw the vast barracks in which they had been housed. Each family had for its dwelling a narrow though lofty cell (one cannot call it a room), lit by a tiny window high up in the wall. Often, as many as seven or eight pairs of lungs inhabited these cells, and the allowance of space was supposed to be seven cubic feet for each person.

The factory was well-lit by electricity. There was
no artificial light in the barracks, and the sanitary
arrangements were unspeakable. One could visualize
in these crowded cells the dingy lives of the powerless
human tools who had ground out profits for the
owners of the mill. The will of one irresponsible
man, backed by State, Church and police, had ruled
the lives of this community. In servitude and
degradation it had made wealth for strangers.

The Revolution attained one negative result in
its first week. The company which had owned
Sóbinka vanished like a fiction. The powerful
personality who had founded it fled to some haunt
of exiles. The State, with its armed force, stood
now behind the workers. Here in this lonely clearing
in the forest the herd of workers became a self-
governing community. It made plans. It began to
adapt its environment to its own ends and needs.
It acquired a collective will. As the new manager
(a former artisan) and his expert heads of departments recounted its history, the positive meaning of
the Revolution came home to me. Without training
or experience, amid war, civil war and blockade,
sometimes half-starved and often for long months
without cotton, grappling with every imaginable
difficulty, material and moral, this community had
striven, as its own master, to lay the foundations
of a human and autonomous life.

Some achievements lay to its credit, and in these
one may read its purpose. It had installed electric
light in the barrack-dwellings, and the pipes lay
ready for the introduction of drains. It had created
crèches and kindergartens—simple, indeed, but clean
and kindly—under qualified nurses and teachers, for
all the younger children. The inadequate old school

was working "double shifts." By day it belonged
to the children. In the evening it was crowded with
classes for the youths and the illiterate adults,
including nearly four hundred women. Six of the
technical staff of the mill had conducted classes
to instruct the younger men in the science of
weaving. A library had somehow been collected,
with nine hundred volumes. A small theatre had
been erected, a graceful building of wood, and
here an amateur choir, a band, a dramatic club
and a cinematograph—all of them new—gave
frequent performances. Plans of real artistic merit
had been drawn for new workers' dwellings, and
the material for their erection lay ready for use.
The timber had been cut by the workers themselves in the brief interval of early spring,
between Deníkin's defeat and the Polish attack,
and then the work had stopped, for Sóbinka,
its population now reduced to about 3,200 active
workers, had given no less than 1,200 of these to
the Red Army. When the civil war cut off the oil
and coal fuel, Sóbinka had to resort to the forest
and the peat bogs. Eight hundred men without
horses (for these had been mobilized) cut the logs
and the turf and carried them in hand-carts. They
were just completing a narrow-gauge railway to the
turf fields four miles away, and I saw part of it
in use. Much of their energy during the summer
drought had been engaged in fighting the continual
forest fires, and they had trained a fire brigade, which
gave in my presence a most creditable exhibition of
its efficiency. Finally, it should be mentioned (though
this was the work of the provincial Soviet) that a
corps of engineers, whom I saw at work, even at the
height of the Polish War, was replacing the floating

causeways with well-built bridges, and the river will soon be navigable.

The chronicle of work is soon told, but, emphasize it as I may, it cannot impress the reader as it impresses me. One must have lived in the Russia of to-day to realize how much contrivance and perseverance it takes to do the simplest piece of constructive work. For the crèches and kindergartens young women who had never seen either must be trained by instructors who themselves knew as little some months before. If digging has to be done, you must first make your spade, and usually of wood. That pipes, rails and electric fittings could be provided, in a country which before the war rarely made any of these things, implied an economic miracle. I gave to a communal farm a packet of nails and screws which had cost me a few shillings in London. As the men thanked me, they told me that they could not have bought them in Russia with tens of thousands of roubles. In spite of all this, the factory at Sóbinka had built and improved its estate. The will to create was alive : the stimulus of freedom was stirring the collective will of thousands who before the Revolution had been the passive tools of the employer, the one person who in that place had the power to plan and decide. There are in Soviet Russia hundreds and thousands of men and women, formerly of the middle class, who are needlessly and unjustifiably hampered and cramped. But to the manual worker the Revolution has brought the power to will and act.

The rest of the story of Sóbinka is less cheerful. "Have we evicted the mill along with the owner ? " I heard one workman say, half in earnest, half in jest. Sóbinka depended for its cotton on the supplies of Turkestan, and these had varied with the vicissitudes of the civil war.   First the Czecho-Slovaks and then Deníkin had occupied the railways and the rivers which should have carried its supplies, and even after their defeat the broken bridges and the wrecked traffic yards had first to be repaired.   The result of this isolation was that Turkestan, during the civil war, ceased to grow its unmarketable cotton.   The area sown actually fell in 1919 to less than one-eighth of what it was in 1916.   The farmers took to growing cereals and potatoes instead of cotton, and the model plantations were ruined. The quality also declined, and the staple is now only half its former average length.   There has been a rapid improvement during 1920 under Soviet rule in Turkestan, and the crop is now about one-half of the pre-war average.   These conditions in Turkestan were naturally reflected at Sóbinka. Months of idleness or short time had alternated with months of work.   From April to September, cotton had wholly failed, partly, I think, because the railways were busy with military transport.   At last, supplies for two months had arrived, and on the day of my visit all hands were engaged in cleaning and oiling the wonderful machines (among the best in Russia), preparatory to re-starting.   An English foreman, a veteran from Lancashire, who had refused all offers of repatriation because he " would not desert the ship in difficulties," told me that spinners and weavers were both skilful and industrious, and I gathered that the discipline of work was now satisfactory, but everyone is on half rations, and for the weakened hands and the tired nerves the old output is impossible.   The official reckoning assumes only 60 per cent. of the former output as a minimum. A policy of payment by premium will reward anything over this low standard by increments of the money payments, which may go up to a tripled wage for a doubled output.

The factory has been promised food rations on the so-called " armoured " scale. If that is really available punctually and in full measure, the workers will be adequately fed. But even so, the factory will not yield its old output. The Workers' Council has decided that not more than three persons, instead of the former seven or eight, shall live in each of those cramped cells in the old barracks. That still means, by any civilized standard, gross overcrowding, but the result, until the new dwellings are completed, is that instead of the old 12,000, Sóbinka can now house only about 4,800 workers with their children. At the best it will hardly approach half its pre-war output, and if the Army continues to absorb (as it has hitherto done) the whole of the cloth it produces, there remains no margin whatever to pay for the workers' food.

In this factory in the forest the baffling problem of Revolutionary Russia is already stated. One felt the force of the explosive deed which had shattered an intolerable oppression. One saw at work the creative will, which by some miracle of buoyancy and optimism, insists on building and constructing amid hunger and nakedness. One realized sadly that it had created everything but prosperity. One understood in some measure why it had failed, as one counted the tale of workers absent at the front and caught a glimpse, across two thousand miles of railway, of those cotton fields which war had put out of

2

cultivation. Russia has hardly yet begun to create her dream of a Communist economy. She has only struggled to survive amid war, civil war and blockade. One thing, however, she has done. She has broken the power of autocratic wealth to order the lives of men.

CHAPTER II

CLOTH FROM CORN

A CLEVER new cartoon caught my eye in Petrograd as I was leaving Russia. On the left of the drawing a big giant of a peasant stood pouring, with lavish hands, a sack of corn into the hopper of a mill. On the right another peasant smilingly received an armful of cloth and boots which came pouring out of the mill. "How to get cloth from corn," ran the legend under the drawing. That, in one phrase, is the whole of Russia's problem to-day. The foreign investigator is curious about many things. He wants to assess the gain and loss in the Soviet system. He is curious about the rival politics of Bolsheviks and Mensheviks. He is critical of the dictatorship of the Communist party. He soon learns, however, if he is sensitive to the mental atmosphere around him, that these things are to-day the concern only of the small minority which is still politically minded. The politics of Russia turn on only one question, how to break the vicious circle of industry and food. By some magic she must get corn for the weavers that there may be cloth for the peasants. Every expedient has been tried. Somehow to drill or galvanize or bribe the half-fed workers into producing for the peasants more textiles and boots is one possible way, but as soon as the goods are ready, the Army claims them. Somehow to persuade or coerce the peasant into lending corn, in the hope that better-fed workers will repay the debt in cloth, is another possible way; but again, when success is near, it is the Army that eats the grain. The problem cannot be solved without peace, nor without the lifting of the blockade. It is mainly a question of external policy. It was one of the ablest of the few leading Communists who said to me : " What can our foreign policy be, but to secure as many railway engines and agricultural machines as possible ? "

If it was true this year that food is the question of questions, one fears that next year anxiety may become tragedy. Hitherto, since the Revolution, Nature had been Bolshevik, for all Russia had a series of good harvests. This summer came the drought, such a drought as Russia has not known since the famine of 1891. The yield of all crops in Central Russia is about 40 per cent. of the normal. In the Eastern Ukraine, the standing corn was literally burned by the sun. The survival of the towns depends on the few regions, all distant, and all inclined to be disaffected, where the harvest has been good—the Kuban Cossack district, the West Ukraine and further Siberia. These catastrophes need not occur, if agriculture were even moderately scientific.

I saw one experimental farm belonging to the Vladímir Soviet, which, from the usual sandy soil, under the same rainless skies, had reaped the best harvest for seven years, thanks mainly to deep ploughing. The Bolsheviks have turned all the tremendous resources of their machinery of agitation and education to the task of teaching the peasant some of the first elements of good cultivation. But the distance to be travelled is immense. Arthur Young, at the end of the eighteenth century, was horrified at the prevalence of the three-field system in England and France. Round Vladímir I found that the usual scheme of cultivation was a two-field system. Half the soil lay fallow every year, and the fallow field was not even weeded. Beans and turnips, lucerne, and even clover, were almost unknown. Potatoes and cabbages were the only common crops, besides the staple grain and flax. The sandy soil was only scratched upon the surface, and when drought came, the crops were starved. It came in the tropical heat of this rainless summer like a scourge. I saw ripe flax that stood less than a foot above the ground, and over the dry forest there hung an endless pall of smoke. Even the cut turf would sometimes catch fire. Of one fact let me remind the reader who thinks of Russia as a grain-exporting country. The surplus came solely from the Ukraine, the Volga Valley, the Caucasus and Siberia. Central and Northern Russia were never, at the best of times, self-supporting, and it is only over these regions, which always have, and always had, a food deficit, that Bolshevik rule has been uninterrupted. Their problem was to feed a country which never in Tsarist days had come near to feeding itself.

It is hard to give an accurate and objective account of the degree in which the Soviet Government has succeeded, in spite of war, civil war and blockade, in feeding Central Russia.[1] My own view of this,

[1] The official statistics of the grain supply show year by year a rapid improvement in the amounts actually

and, indeed, of the whole economic problem, is more favourable than that of most English visitors. It happens that I am used to black bread, and like it, and I found the Russian workman's staple dish, " kasha " (any porridge of buckwheat, millet, oats or barley), both nourishing and palatable. But I have heard a kindly English Labour leader describing " kasha " as food fit only for animals. There is some truth in a retort which Radek made in my hearing : " You Englishmen think that you are starved unless you have fish for breakfast." By English standards the condition of Russia is certainly appalling, but so it always was, if one takes the lot of the working class into account. My own rule was to ignore English standards entirely, and to compare Russia with blockaded Central Europe as I saw it last year. Allowing for the fact that Russia was always less orderly, less civilized and vastly poorer,

requisitioned and stored by the Government. These amounts were :

    1917–18, 80 million poods (62 poods are 1 ton)
    1918–19, 106   „   „
    1919–20, 156   „   „
    1920–21, 454   „   „   (estimated).

The available figures for 1920, which I have only for August and September, show that the estimate was greatly exceeded. Apparently an increased quantity is being obtained from Siberia and the Northern Caucasus, which balances the failure of the harvest elsewhere. The figure estimated for the present year is about half the yearly supply of the Russian internal market (900 millions) in pre-war days, but I presume that figure included Poland, the Baltic Provinces and Finland. In other words, allowing for this loss of territory and for the decline of the urban population, the town-dwellers may hope for something approaching an adequate food supply. But I gravely doubt this estimate.

the comparison was, on the whole, to the advantage of Russia.[1]

*   *   *   *   *

To be sure, Petrograd looks at a first glance like a dead city. Grass grows literally in the streets, and I even saw a wild flower here and there. Hamburg quays in the latter years of the war were in the same condition. Petrograd was, in the industrial sense, always an artificial creation. It depended on sea-borne English coal and American cotton, with rubber and other imported raw materials. Its decay began long before the Revolution, and it is lucky that only about 600,000 remain of its former two million inhabitants. The mortality must have

[1] I find confirmation of this opinion in the monthly *Record* of the Save the Children Fund for October. It gives a shaded map indicating the comparative needs of different parts of Europe. The two black patches, oddly enough, are also politically the " whitest." They are (1) Poland and the Crimea, with some territory to the north of it, held at that date by Baron Wrangel. (2) After these two regions of " greatest distress " come German Austria, parts of Czecho-Slovakia and the Baltic Republics, marked " great distress among children." (3) Next we have a lightly shaded region, covering the greater part of Germany, marked " general shortage and distress." (4) Finally, in the least distressed category (" badly in need of clothing, drugs, etc.") there are Hungary, Jugo-Slavia, and the whole of Soviet Russia. The big towns, however, are in this map treated separately, and on its showing there seems to be little to choose in their plight. Vienna, Budapest, Warsaw, Berlin, Leipzig and, indeed, all the bigger German towns, are placed in either the first or the second category of gravest distress. Petrograd and Moscow are placed in the first (worst) class, and Kiev, Kharkóv and Sarátov in the second. As a whole, then, on this evidence, Soviet Russia is much less distressed than Central Europe, while its towns are in much the same condition.

been heavy, but on the whole, most of the vanished population has returned to its native villages. The old wooden houses of the slums, infested with vermin and reeking of disease, have been pulled down, partly as a sanitary measure and partly to furnish fuel. Here and there in the wood-paved streets one even noticed holes where the blocks had been stolen for fuel. One rarely saw horses in the streets, probably because they had been eaten. " Petrograd," as a Russian wit has said, " is paradise. Here men eat apples and go naked." The city looked unspeakably dreary with its closed shops and its deserted streets, while the pitiless northern light revealed the crumbling stucco and faded paint of its grandiose Italian palaces. Its fate, I imagine, is to be a northern Ghent, a superb architectural monument to a vanished past. It will begin to recover, as the chief port of the North, only when trade is resumed. Its harbour has been renovated this summer, but no ship has entered it.

None the less, Petrograd, stricken first by the German and then by the Allied blockade, is less pitiable than Vienna, though it has lived solely by " self-help." It is not nearly so dead as one imagines on the first view. It maintains a sadly diminished industry, with wood instead of English coal as its fuel. Its mental life is active. The walls are covered with placards which announce innumerable courses of lectures for working men. It boasts that in three months of this year its adult schools succeeded in halving the number of grown-up illiterates in the population. The theatre and the opera are always crowded. Moscow, on the other hand, makes on the stranger who has passed through Petrograd a much less dismal impression. Petrograd was pri-

marily a capital and a port. To-day it is neither.
Moscow, on the contrary, has returned to its
traditional position. It is the capital once more,
and the Kremlin is no longer an antiquity, but the
heart of Russia's life. The streets are animated,
and at certain hours even crowded. There has been,
here also, a reduction of the population, but only
on a relatively small scale. There are still cabs
in considerable numbers plying for hire. As you
grow familiar with the streets, even the closed shops
impress you less. For one thing, you realize that
they are not really absolutely closed. You may
pass a shop four or five times and find it closed.
The sixth time, a queue is standing at the door.
You learn on inquiry that the rather complicated
system of ration cards gives to each working citizen
the right to expend a certain maximum sum per
month upon goods of which only a limited quantity
exists—crockery, glass and hardware, for example.
Every day the newspapers announce that cards
bearing certain numbers may be used in certain
shops. If you need the articles in question, you
take your place in the queue. The things, when
you do receive them, are, when one takes the
infinitesimal value of the rouble into account,
ridiculously cheap. The trouble is that there are
not nearly enough to go round. The card system,
however, ensures an equitable distribution. Every
trade union (and all working citizens, including
members of the learned professions, belong to a
trade union) has also a committee to which one
may apply if one is in urgent need, say of boots,
an overcoat, or an English Dictionary. These things
are all desperately scarce, and orders entitling you
to buy (at the " dirt-cheap " Soviet prices) are given

only if you can prove your need. Railway tickets are dispensed on the same principle, as they were for a time in Germany. Shopping, in short, is a cumbersome process, and the difficulty of dispensing the poverty-stricken stocks to each according to his need, has led to the growth of a complicated bureaucratic system. When I realized how much energy one must expend to buy a collar or a pair of socks, I was less favourably impressed by the activity of the crowds in the streets. But the shops are much more active than one supposes at a first glance. One big multiple store in Moscow, which is open all day, has an average of 15,000 customers daily. In Moscow a great deal of speculative " free trade " is still tolerated. You may see the old spirit of mercantile gain untrammelled and unregenerate on market-days. The biggest of the markets (the Sucharévka) is a crowded study in need and greed. Prosperous peasants are selling milk, butter and vegetables at prices which sound fabulous in roubles, but are in reality, given the exchange, much the same as those at home. The dealers no longer trouble to say that such an article costs so many thousand roubles. They quote it at " two " or " three," and the thousand is understood. A thousand roubles is now worth about two shillings, which used to be the value of one. Beside them stand reduced gentlewomen, selling what remains of their laces and furs. At one stall you may see metal articles, made by Soviet workmen, I regret to say, on Soviet lathes and with odds and ends of Soviet metal, to supplement their wages. Pickpockets, often mere children, glide about actively in the dense crowd. If you want to be robbed and cheated, expeditiously and in the old-fashioned way, there is still every facility for the experience in Moscow.

Petrograd has abolished the open market, and its food administration is said to be the most capable in Russia. Speculation in food has been driven underground, which means that most of the available supply can be bought at the Soviet prices. A "Soviet" loaf costs two roubles, which is nothing at all, with wages ranging from 2,000 to 8,000 roubles a month. The "speculative" loaf of black bread costs 400 roubles in Moscow, which has a much less efficient local administration. In both cities there is a free dinner available for every citizen, man or woman. The menu may be scanty and the cooking, to my notions, was usually bad, but there were millions last year in Poland, Austria and even Germany who would have rejoiced at a diet of cabbage soup, barley "kasha," a roast apple and a glass of tea, even once a day. I had grown familiar with the drooping gait, the lagging steps, the grey skin and the white lips of the crowds in Vienna streets. I noticed nothing of the kind in Moscow, or even in Petrograd. Men and women walked immense distances in both these scattered cities, for the electric "tram" cars were overcrowded and infrequent, but they tramped for the most part sturdily enough. Nor was that only my own impression. I met both Germans and Austrians in Moscow who all remarked on the obviously better physical condition of the Russian workers as compared with their own. Above all, the children in Russia are on the whole happy, and even relatively well-fed. In Russia there is no parallel to the tragedy of child life which is the worst of all the plagues of Central Europe.

Nor was it only in the matter of health and food

that Russia seemed to me more fortunate than
Central Europe. Transport is still the gravest of
Russian problems. There might, with the best
management, be just enough locomotives in Russia
to deal with the indispensable civilian traffic. There
are not nearly enough to conduct a war on two
fronts and to serve the cities as well. There is,
indeed, a steady if slow improvement. There was in
February only one " healthy " locomotive for every
twelve versts of the railway system. Thanks to the
tremendous efforts of the repairing shops, there was,
in August, one sound engine to every eight versts.
The pre-war standard, however, was one engine to
three versts. This problem, then, is still far from its
solution, and no great change is likely, until the
Allies so far raise the financial blockade as to permit
Russia to purchase spare parts for locomotives.
None the less, it seemed to me that this nation,
which has spontaneously so little conception of order
and punctuality, had been drilled, first by Krassin
and then by Trotsky, on the railways into a very
creditable measure of system. I found the ordinary
Russian passenger trains, even when wood was the
fuel, quicker, more punctual and more comfortable
than most of those in which I travelled in Central
Europe last year. The time-table was always observed, and the amount of time spent at each stopping
place was, through better organization, a mere
fraction of what is usual even now in Esthonia.
There is a regular train which reaches Irkutsk, in
far Siberia, from Moscow in seven days, while an
express runs twice a week from Moscow to the
Caucasus in sixty hours. Troop trains move on an
average faster than was usual in the Great War.
Two years ago the railways were a chaos. They

are to-day a creditable achievement in the art of making the most of sadly limited materials.

*   *   *   *   *

To compare the food supply of Russia with that of Central Europe is, however, to take a very low standard. Everyone knows, or ought to know, that the maximum legal allowance of food by ration cards in Germany and Austria is less than half the physiological minimum necessary for health. Even this minimum is far above the unskilled worker's wage. The chief difficulty in judging Russian conditions is to strike some mean among their bewildering variety. The peasants, to begin with, are certainly better off in most respects than they were before. I talked with many peasant delegates in the Vladímir Soviet, as well as with chance peasants in the villages. All agreed that they had enough to eat, and even that everyone in the village had enough. I have seen statistics collected last year by a group of Russian economists which put the fact beyond a doubt. The peasant, even the poorest peasant of the sterile central regions, is living better and eating more than ever before. I was a guest several times in peasant houses and in communal or " Soviet " farms. The abundance and good quality of the food was in some of them surprising, even if one assumes that the generous hospitality traditional in Russia had spread an unusually lavish table. One saw at some of these peasant tables the things which the townsman can obtain only at extravagant speculative prices— butter and honey, poultry and fish. A glance at the outside of a village tells its own tale. The peasants are building, and building rather extensively. Everywhere one saw new houses, and they were usually bigger and better constructed than the old. Again, the official statistics of the livestock in the Vladímir Province, which happens to be a relatively poor district, showed that its total possessions in horned cattle had increased appreciably since the year of the Revolution.   Industrial Russia has passed, and is still passing, through a painful crisis of adaptation.   Rural Russia, save in the more savagely devastated districts, is obviously and certainly more prosperous than ever before.   This green Russia, be it remembered, outnumbers industrial Russia in population by nearly ten to one.

There are, however, certain drawbacks to this relative prosperity of the country-side.   There are some necessary or usual articles of food which the farmer cannot supply.   In many parts of Russia salt was almost unobtainable throughout this summer. I saw one village market in a western province at which most of the peasant women who had poultry, eggs, milk and fruit to dispose of, refused to part with anything for money.   I tried hard to buy, only to receive the monotonous answer, " For salt." A sucking-pig could be had for two pounds of salt. Vladímir had just received a year's supply of salt as I left it, but the distribution had not yet begun.

Sugar, again, of which Russians habitually consume an enormous amount with their continual glasses of weak tea, almost disappeared while the Ukraine was in Deníkin's occupation.   " Last year," as one Soviet official put it, " we simply forgot the taste of it."   The Vladímir Soviet did much for apiculture this summer by distributing hives and bees, but not yet on a sufficient scale.   An inventor, himself a Petrograd working man, discovered a process by which sugar can be extracted from sawdust—preferably from birchwood.   The product was satisfactory, but it was never available in sufficient quantities.   It is roughly true to say that sugar reappeared in the official ration only for some four months after the recovery of the Ukraine, and then all but disappeared again, save for children, as the Polish War disorganized transport.

Even more serious from the peasants' standpoint was the total lack of lamp oil during last winter.   The reason was, of course, that Deníkin's army held the roads to Baku, and a small British force controlled the oilfield.   The dreary months of darkness had somehow to be passed without artificial light.   The more enterprising peasants usually carry on a handicraft during winter, and more especially in the evenings.   Some are half-time carpenters, some bootmakers, others potters.   The Soviets have done much to encourage these home industries, and an exhibition at Vladímir showed, besides the familiar Russian carved toys, some admirable hand-made furniture, solid, tasteful and well-finished—an entirely new departure.   Some of these village craftsmen talked bitterly of their experiences last winter, when the working day ended indoors in darkness towards three or four o'clock.   This privation, however, will not recur, for oil is once more coming steadily up the Volga from Baku, and in the Vladímir province a stock had arrived which would allow a generous supply (216 pounds) to each peasant house.

The dire need of clothing and boots affects the entire Russian population, rural as well as urban. The peasants usually have their sheepskin coats, and in some villages the art of growing, spinning and weaving flax is still practised.   None the less, it was always of the lack of clothes that the peasants complained most bitterly. Everything was short, from sewing cotton, needles and buttons to the top-boots which the peasant specially affects. As usual in Russia, the children fared best. A supply of 80 yards of textiles is given to the mother for each new-born child. Every child in the schools of Vladímir province received 6 yards of textiles for one year. Industrial workers in Vladímir received 20 yards for one year, with 12 yards for the members of their families. The peasants received much less— 7½ yards for each man, woman and child. The word "textiles" means, however, only cotton or linen. No heavier cloth and no wool or flannel was distributed. The case with boots was even worse. There are sixteen teachers, for example, in the "middle" school of Vladímir. They received among them two pairs of boots and two pairs of goloshes last winter. A teacher of the highest grade who tried to buy a pair of boots in the speculative market, would have had to spend five months' salary upon them (40,000 roubles). Even in the Foreign Office at Moscow last winter only 60 per cent. of the staff received any footwear at all, and only 30 per cent. got boots. One did not notice the lack of clothing much during the tropical summer. Linen and cotton are fairly plentiful, and the young women in the streets were often becomingly dressed. Even their fashion of going barelegged, with little socks and light shoes, looked enviable in the great heat. Rain and even snow came, however, before I left, and it was pitiful to realize that most of the working women had nothing better to wear than a single cotton skirt. All the warm cloth, all the heavy great-coats and all the top-boots had gone to the Red Army, which, like all armies, wears out these things prodigally. Soap is a costly luxury. None at all was distributed in the provinces : the scanty supplies just sufficed for the hospitals, crèches and schools.

* * * * *

The inability of the Soviet Government to supply salt, sugar, paraffin, soap, boots and warm clothing to the peasants, not to mention nails and tools, in anything like adequate quantities, explains in part the dearth of food. The peasant gave up his surplus grain reluctantly, because he got no sufficient return in kind. This initial difficulty was redoubled by the difficulties of transport due to incessant war. The rich agricultural regions of Russia (Siberia, Ukraine and Caucasus) lie all of them on the furthest margins of the Republic, which means a terrific strain upon the railways, which carry the grain inwards and the manufactures outwards, to and from the industrial centre. It is, moreover, in Central Russia that the strength of Communism lies. Petrograd, Moscow and the Central Provinces yielded a Bolshevik majority even at the elections for the Constituent Assembly in 1917, whereas the distant provinces at the best only acquiesce, and there the lightest requisition is risky.

The result may be studied in the following table. I obtained it from the evidently honest and capable officials of the Vladímir Soviet, and found it accurate, whenever I tested it by supplementary inquiries. It gives for each category of the population the amount of flour, or its equivalent in bread, theoretically due, and then the amount actually distributed between March and August of this year. The curious term " armoured " workers covers those in munition

3

factories, mines and certain textile factories working
for the Army, who are supposed to receive extra
food. The second category includes officials, clerks
and other sedentary workers :

Standard.	" Armoured " Workers, 36 lb.	Other Workers, 25 lb.	Workers' Families (Adults), 18 lb.	Children (Average), 15–30 lb. according to Age.
March ..	25	25	18	15
April	11	11	5½	10
May	10	10	5	9
June	14	7	8	12
July	15	10	4	13
August ..	10½	10½	6	10

The reader who studies this table will realize at
once that he has before him a summary sketch of
conditions which approach those of a besieged city
in the last stages of its resistance. The standard,
to begin with, is low. The Red Army normally
received two pounds of bread daily, and this is about
what the Russian manual worker expects, unless he
is well supplied with meat, fish or kasha. The actual
amount supplied fell in some categories to the merest
fraction of the standard. Vladímir, I think, was
typical of Central Russia. Petrograd fared better,
but Moscow was in much the same plight. On the
Volga supplies were, I believe, ampler. It may seem
a miracle that any population can survive upon this
diet. In reality, the facts were never so bad as this
table suggests.

To begin with, the daily public dinner was available
for the entire urban population—free in the two

capitals and at a nominal charge in provincial towns. For children there was always one free meal, and sometimes two. Again, nearly everyone belonged to some co-operative society, usually connected with his office or workshop, which was authorized to buy country produce, often as far afield as Siberia. This " co-operative " food was sold at prices well within the worker's income. Again, many of the town workers, especially in Petrograd and in the smaller towns, had " allotments " and potato patches. The railwaymen even grew rye for their own use. But the struggle was very sharp. The women teachers told me that they supplemented their incomes by dressmaking. Much was winked at which was highly irregular. Metal workers, for example, would make automatic lighters from Government material and sell them in the speculative market. Tobacco workers were allowed 1,500 cigarettes monthly, which they usually sold. Want, under-nourishment and anxiety were the lot of everyone. None the less, it was a common remark, even in hostile circles in Vladímir, that no one is now actually dying of hunger. Typhus, which always comes with famine, had not recurred this year, though in 1919 no less than 3 per cent. of the town population of Vladímir suffered from it. Typhoid, thanks to a better water supply, was actually less prevalent than before the war. The vital statistics were only a little less terrible than those of Central European towns. The birth-rate, taking the industrial population only, had fallen from a pre-war 41 to 30 per 1,000—a drop which medical opinion ascribed partly to the mobilization of the men. The urban death-rate had risen in this same Vladímir province from a pre-war 27 to about 50 per 1,000. Let me emphasize

once more that these grave conditions affected only
the urban minority in Russia.

The worst part of its suffering was due to the
war. The monthly table tells its own tale. In
March, with an adequate food supply, Russia was
nearer to peace than she has ever been, before or
since, during six long years. The Polish offensive had
not yet begun and the Western frontier was held only
by a thin screen of troops. Deníkin had disappeared
and Wrangel held only the Crimean peninsula. The
Army was partly demobilized and partly transformed
into labour battalions. Everyone, from Lenin downwards, believed that peace had actually come. A
rage for construction and peaceful work seized every
Soviet. At last they started to realize the grandiose
ambition of transforming Russia into a civilized
Republic, with the will of its workers for its motive
force. Even in this brief three months of respite
much was done, even in quiet, backward Vladímir,
to transform the neglected estate inherited from
Tsardom. Here schools were built, there bridges.
I saw one village in which electric light had been
installed.[1] One must have seen a village in Central
Russia to grasp the whole meaning of such a portent.
Nothing had changed in this long street of log cabins
since first there were Tsars in Moscow. And now
the engineers came from Vladímir town, erected a
wooden turbine in the water-mill, installed a dynamo
and laid their cables. At first, the peasants shook
their heads. Some prophesied that it would not
work ; others said, " Such things are only for the
gentry." The really clever people were of opinion

---

[1] Since the Revolution, eight small towns and fifty-nine
villages have been electrified in the Vladímir province. Before
the Revolution there was electricity only in Vladímir city.

that the electric " fluid " could not possibly run up the hill from the mill to the village. When at last the light blazed in every cottage, the neighbouring villages came to beg for their share in the miracle. Nor was this all. The first steps were taken in a big scheme of railway building, to link up all the isolated forest factories by narrow-gauge lines to the main system. The munition factories had actually begun to plan their own transformation to peaceful tasks. The manager of one big powder-mill confided to me that he had everything ready to start the manufacture of writing-paper and artificial silk at a few weeks' notice.

Then at a sign from Paris the Poles struck their blow. Interrupted in their happy constructive work, the young men were summoned and entrained for Kiev. No experience of a Western land can give even a faint conception of the loss in man-power which mobilization involves in Russia. With us, the young men between twenty and thirty-five may be more energetic than their elders, but they are not appreciably more intelligent or even much better educated. In Russia the difference is almost that between two distinct races. All the energy, all the faith, all the will, and, among the workers, nearly all the education, belong to the young. The elders, especially in the country, are passive, lethargic, indolent, illiterate, as only Russians can be. Among the mobilized were practically all the clever young workmen, mainly Communists, who in the new schools for administrators, officers and teachers have received their training for their responsibilities in a workers' republic. Not one of these was left in Vladímir; they were all at the front. Even of the heads of local Soviet administration all the

ablest had been transferred to the front. That was
one consequence of the war. The other is legible
in the food statistics. As the railways adapted
themselves to the dispatch of endless troop trains
from the Far South and the Far East to the Far
West, the food supply of Central Russia sank to a
fraction of the standard.

CHAPTER III

A SOVIET IN SESSION

I WAS lucky during my stay in Vladímir to find the provincial Soviet in session. The little town with its 40,000 inhabitants, some hundred and twenty miles due east of Moscow, is like many another capital of a " gubérnia " (province) in Central Russia. I used to fancy that it might have been the model for Gogol's country town in *The Inspector-General*—the place from which you might drive for three years and never reach a frontier. Nature, however, had made it more picturesque than most Russian towns, for in this land of endless plains it stood on a low ridge of hills. Below it wound the gleaming serpentine stream of the River Klyasma, and from the height one saw the endless Central Russian forest stretching to the horizon, its green dimmed by the menacing pall of smoke from the incessant fires. Vladímir, moreover, has a distinguished past. Its two cathedrals date from the twelfth century, and one of them, an odd square building, covered with fantastic reliefs of birds, beasts, Saints and their Creator, is familiar to students of architecture. At one end of its long main street stands the " golden gate," a

triumphal arch, built by local princes before there
was a Tsar in Moscow.

The Revolution had changed little in its outer
aspect. Most of the shops, indeed, were closed,
though tantalizing advertisements still promised the
non-existent goloshes or hats. The few Soviet
stores were generally " sold out " and deserted
before midday. The uneven streets were comparatively clean. Two motor-cars existed in the whole
province—there had been none before the war—
and all the horses shied at them, so primitive is
this place. The electric light blazed in the streets
for three hours after nightfall, a luxury rarer
in Moscow. The usual efforts of Communist propaganda, posters in colour, posters in print and clever
stencilled drawings, imprinted in black on the
whitewashed walls, formed your mind for you,
as you walked, by their reiterated suggestion. The
little town was monotonously orderly, puritanical
and quiet. In my two weeks' stay I never saw a
drunken man, a prostitute or a game of cards. I
neither witnessed nor heard of a single act of violence or roughness. A very few armed militiamen
patrolled the streets, but I never heard a shot,[1]

---

[1] This remark may sound absurd to the Western reader.
I was thinking of sleepless nights spent last year in Polish
towns, with rifle fire crackling intermittently from dusk to
dawn. The Polish gendarmes and sentries held that a rifle
was meant for use. There were also days in Warsaw when
formidable batteries of guns would take up position at
strategical street-corners, if the unemployed were expected
to demonstrate. In Lodz the mounted police charged up
and down the streets with lances. It occurs to me that I
have forgotten to make the necessary remark that Soviet
Russia is quite as orderly as England and much more orderly
than Poland.

and in a conspicuous place there stood a letter-box
specially set apart and labelled for " Complaints
against the Militia." I used to wonder in this
" Bolshevik chaos " what order looks like in Cork.

The Soviet met, at least thrice a year, in a big
classical building which had been the Nobles' Club.
One could imagine the brilliant balls of the old
regime. To-day the place has become a " district
club," and hundreds of serious, well-behaved working-class youths, including soldiers, throng it every
evening to hear lectures or to listen to good concerts
of classical or Russian music. The gilded chairs
of the big assembly hall were a little dingy, and in
a heavy frame, surmounted by an Imperial eagle
shrouded in red, a poor portrait of Lenin in oils had
replaced what doubtless was an equally poor portrait
of Tsar Nicholas. Much, no doubt, had been lost
in elegance and the surface refinements of manner ;
but I doubt if anything is lost to civilization. By
all accounts the nobles dined well, danced well and
played high in this club, but it is not recorded that
they listened to lectures on history or economics.
The outer aspect of the Soviet was rather sombre.
There was a group of half a dozen women members
from textile factories. All the rest were obviously
workmen or peasants, big men, roughly dressed,
and I think the only " intellectuals " among them
were one or two village teachers. There the history
of this revolution was made visible. In its first
months the " intellectuals " had combated it with
an organized boycott. Their passive resistance was
gradually broken. For nearly two years they had
endured what was at best a suspicious tolerance.
It was only towards the end of 1919 that the word
of order came from the centre for a sort of recon-

ciliation. Their food ration had been raised and their opportunities of service increased. Many of them have responded in loyal and devoted work. The class cleavage, however, remains. They are not trusted by the workmen. They are not welcomed in the governing Communist party. They are rarely elected to the Soviets. They are still only the employees of the dominant proletariat.

The Vladímir Soviet, like every other, contained an overwhelming majority of Communists (Bolsheviks). There were no Mensheviks who sat under that name. A tiny opposition, very loyal and discreet, perhaps 10 per cent. of the whole body, sheltered under the " non-party " label. There is much discussion among advanced circles in the West as to the relative merits of an occupational as opposed to a territorial franchise. The question has its theoretical interest, but there is little light on it to be derived from Russian practice. The plain historic fact is that the Soviet was evolved as a fighting organization, well adapted to conduct a general strike. It remains in being as an organ of the Communist dictatorship. To waste time in discussing it as a representative system would be either foolish or dishonest. Under a dictatorship which denies, even to the tolerated Menshevik opposition, the indispensable opportunities of propaganda through the Press and public meeting, no system of representation can work as such. By one expedient or another, the opposition is kept within insignificant dimensions, and the Soviet " represents " only the Communist party. No Russian Bolshevik would dispute or resent that plain statement of fact. It is the non-Russian propagandists who obscure the truth. None the less, it is possible

that, even under free and equal conditions, the
Communists, unless food at the moment were specially
scarce, could secure a majority in Vladímir. They
polled in this province 55 per cent. of the
votes in the " democratic " elections for the Constituent Assembly in 1917—as, indeed, they did
throughout Central Russia. They have, since then,
increased their influence among the younger
generation.

The debates, given the somewhat artificial origin
of the Soviet as a body virtually nominated by the
Communist party, surprised me agreeably by their
vigour and spirit. Of politics in our Western sense
of the word one heard little. Some hours were
occupied by a very long report on the Polish War,
the London negotiations and the economic prospects of the Republic, by a member of the central
administration, Comrade Larin, sent down from
Moscow, according to custom, for this purpose.
The main business consisted in the discussion of
the reports which each of the heads of Departments of the Vladímir government made upon his
own exercise of responsibility. Each report dealt
both with the achievements in the past and the
plans for the future, with much precise detail and
full statistics. The Soviet listened very quietly
and attentively : there was little applause and no
interruption, and many of the delegates took copious
notes in order to be able to report to the county
or district (Uyezd or Volost) councils which had
elected them to the provincial (gubérnia) Soviet.
Most of them were men themselves actively engaged,
in some smaller field, in the work of administration.
Politics mean in Russia to-day mainly the handling
of material things, and most of the discussion turned,

in a business-like way, on the building of bridges
or schools, the making of agricultural machines,
the reorganization of factories and the supply of
essential goods. I found peasants and workmen
much easier to understand than "intellectuals,"
and got a fair idea of some of their speeches. Many
of them were sharply critical of the administration,
and the hardest hitting came from the Communists.
It is a complete mistake to suppose that party
discipline forbids a critical attitude. The hottest
attack was loudly applauded, and by a vote of the
Soviet the time allotted to this speaker was extended
from five minutes to twenty-five. He urged that
" we should not drop into a lazy way of blaming the
blockade and the war for everything," and that more
bridges and schools could have been built if peasant
labour had been called up for the purpose. The
" Minister " (to give him that Western name) retorted
hotly, whereupon a peasant made a delightfully
naïve but sensible and soothing speech, on the text
" We are teaching ourselves how to rule." A teacher
followed with a much applauded plea for more
schools, and an argument that the peasants are so
eager for education that they would gladly have
obeyed a summons to build them. The " Minister's "
answer was a little irrelevant, but deeply interesting.
No less than three thousand men had been embodied
in early spring in the Vladímir government for the
sole purpose of building : every one of them had had
to be sent to the Polish front. The best speaker in
point of form was a peasant, a non-Communist,
who evidently had a real literary gift : he spoke
slowly, forming his phrases carefully, and giving
to them an original and slightly poetical turn. He
was pleading for more scientific agriculture : " War

is the negation of civilization, and yet it had taught us much, for some of us as prisoners had seen in Germany how the Prussians get rich crops from sandy soil even poorer than ours." A Communist answered him that individual peasant cultivation is hopeless : " the peasants look on the Soviet instructors as anti-christs " : the only hope is to develop the communal farms.

The practical importance of this Soviet meeting seemed to me slight. The criticism was never pushed to the point of a vote, though it must have given useful indications to the " Ministers." The time allotted to important points of detail was inadequate ; even less in the way of real control over administration was attained than in our own Parliamentary debates. Educative, however, these meetings doubtless were : the delegates, most of them self-taught, and all of them without experience of administration or of public speaking before 1917, were slowly " teaching themselves how to rule." The relatively reassuring fact to me was that the Communist party, even in the provinces, evidently admits various tendencies and critical groups. The real act of government is performed, usually once a year, when the Communist party decides whom it will nominate for the all-important " ministerial " posts at the head of the several Departments. To judge from these debates, a " Minister " who had shown himself inefficient would certainly be replaced. The real detailed control of administration lies no longer with Soviets at all, but with the novel institution known as the Workers' and Peasants' Inspection. It does not seem to have been described by other visitors to Russia, and, indeed, I would never have heard of it myself, unless I had seen its name over the door of an office, and gone in to ask what it was. Its influence seems to be growing, and when once I had noticed it, I began to realize, from references in the official Press, how immensely important it is. Its printed reports are a mine of curious and highly independent information, and it happens that frequently, or even usually, the elected inspectors are by majority non-Communists.

Corruption, when detected, was severely punished, and a rather elaborate system existed for detecting both corruption and inefficiency. This system of " inspection " supplied the detailed control which the Soviet itself cannot undertake in its short and infrequent sittings. Each " gubérnia " elects a standing " collegiate " of five inspectors, and these in turn engage a staff of specialists. They examine all the plans, estimates and accounts of the departments, watch the work in operation, and make " flying " visits unannounced to factories and bureaucratic departments. They are assisted by delegates, workmen and peasants, elected by the factory councils and the local (Uyezd and Volost) councils, who attend their sittings and accompany their visits of inspection. In this way an independent popular element is brought in to check the bureaucracy. A similar machinery on a smaller scale exists in the county (Uyezd) and the parish (Volost). Again, there is a " Bureau of Complaints," which receives and investigates written protests from individual citizens, who think they have been wronged by officials. Out of 648 complaints, in seven months, in the Vladímir province, 59 were found to be justified, and the grievances were redressed. The proportion seems low, but it may be, as the chief of the bureau explained, that most of the complainants supposed erroneously that they had suffered wrong, because they did not know the law of the new regime. Three of the five persons who acted as the jury of this bureau were non-Communists.

In the intervals of the debates I found the individual delegates eager to talk about their work. One man told me an almost incredible tale about the results achieved in his factory (a powder-mill) since the Revolution. During the Great War it had 17,000 hands on the pay-sheets, and turned out only 50 poods of powder daily. It now, with only 9,000 hands, made 100 poods daily, beside large quantities of other important things. Under the old regime quite half the " hands " had been used as cooks, coachmen and servants to the staff. The staff itself had been reduced by desertion from fifty-four to nine, but these nine had undertaken the scientific instruction of the abler workmen. The workers had themselves built a club-house, a narrow-gauge railway and a brick kiln, and twelve of them had in their spare time repaired a derelict locomotive, which now carries their products to Moscow. I might have doubted this glowing report, had not the delegate pressed me most earnestly and repeatedly to come and see for myself. Unluckily, the distance was too great. Another delegate told me of the affairs of a group of four big cotton-mills. They had raised their production 40 per cent. over the low level of 1918, and would fulfill their programme for the year, if (a serious reservation) the " armoured " food ration arrived punctually. One of these four mills had recently installed electric power, derived from peat. He was full of their partly accomplished work to utilize a more distant peat field in order to electrify a second mill. They, too, were building a light railway. These two men, eager, ambitious, intelligent and bent on big schemes to raise the productivity of industry, were typical of the part played by the Communist worker. Like the Communist volunteers in the Red Army, their rôle is to lead, to stimulate zeal, to quicken the *tempo* of the sluggish Russian pulse and to set the example of sacrifice and unstinting labour, when others would droop from inanition and fatigue. For this zeal, recollect, the reward is not profits, but only the joy in creative work.

In my talks with the peasants I was chiefly anxious to learn their view of the system of requisitions. The peasants pay no taxes, no rent, no interest on mortgages, and usually their miserable little holdings have been enlarged since the Revolution. On the other hand, they must give up the surplus of their crops to the Government, which maintains a monopoly of the trade in grain. Forty pounds of rye per month is allowed for every member of a peasant's family over one year of age, which seems a sufficient average amount. Fodder, oats, flax and potatoes are treated in the same way. The surplus is valued at the Soviet price, which is a mere fraction of the speculative price. Theoretically the peasant ought to be able to buy with the purchase money boots, textiles and the like, also at the nominal Soviet prices, but in practice these goods are scarce and seldom obtainable, and the low money payment, for one-third of the levy, is therefore almost worthless. The peasant is entitled also to receive the value of two-thirds of his requisitioned crops in kind (cotton, oil, salt, etc.), but once more the quantities given are often inadequate. The equation, if the surplus is large, will not balance, and discontent is inevitable. None the less, the poorer peasants, who have rarely any large surplus, suffer little from these requisitions and probably receive much more than they give. They remember only too well their struggles to live in the old days, and they give credit to the Revolution for the change in their lot. Before the Revolution only 16 per cent. of the peasants in Russia produced any surplus whatever of grain for the market, and 52 per cent. produced less than a bare sufficiency of necessary food. Since the Revolution, holdings have been enlarged, but primarily with the aim of making the peasants self-supporting. They will get no great surplus in Central Russia until they alter their methods of cultivation. One big giant of a peasant, a young man with an open and kindly face, a Communist, as the younger men are apt to be, gave me the experience of his little village. It consisted of 223 persons (say forty families) and in rye (the chief crop) had only given up 1,000 pounds as its collective contribution. It will certainly get textiles and paraffin, not to mention free schooling and other State services, which exceed the value of this corn levy many times over. It is the richer peasants, especially in the black-earth zone, where Communism was never strong, who have a grievance, since they grow a big surplus and receive only a fraction of its value in kind. The war, on the whole, eased the requisitions, as the young soldiers came and went on leave. Certain parts of fields were marked off for the levy, and the peasants would say, as they reaped them, " This is for the Comrades " (meaning the absent Red soldiers), and set it aside.

At this point in my talk with the young giant, a bustling elder peasant kept interrupting us. " Now

4

take a new page," he insisted, "for your notes of what I have to say." He was evidently a somewhat richer man. He had cut 120 poods (a pood is 40 pounds) of hay, and had had to give up three poods for the levy. This seemed to him a gross exaction, and he was surprised that I had no sympathy to bestow. His chief personal reason for opposition to the Revolution was, I think, that some time before it, he and some neighbours had clubbed together to buy the forest which served their village. They had paid all but the last instalment of the price, when suddenly the Revolution nationalized their forest. They can still cut all they need for their own use, whether for fuel or for building, but they cannot make a profit by selling to others. He had once worked in a factory "under Englishmen and Germans" and knew "what superior men really are like." As for these Communist leaders and officials, they are "just ordinary workmen," and he "looked down on them." He wished they had all stuck to the "Calculation" Government (he meant "Coalition," i.e. Kérensky) and fought on to the end in the war. Then "they would have been on top, and could have made the Germans pay, and the Allies would have helped them." He was for the Constituent Assembly, but all the same (a little nervously) was a "non-party man." In fact, I think he must have been an active Social Revolutionary.

At this point my talks with the delegates in the tea-room came to an end. An official concert was about to begin. For some time the choir and orchestra had been filing past me to the assembly-room, and the president sent word that they were waiting for my presence to sing the *Internationale*.

I always suffer acutely from that most trivial of
tunes, well as Russians sing it. The rest of the
concert was all pleasure. The orchestra (half
amateur and half military) played surprisingly
well a programme mainly of recent Russian compositions. The choir was a revelation—but if I
were to try to describe Russian singing, the reader
would wonder why I should weary him with politics.
I might answer that one justification of the Revolution is that it is making hundreds of Russians
capable of artistic self-expression where there was
none before.

CHAPTER IV

A PROVINCIAL ADMINISTRATION

THE word " administration " suggests to our Western experience an important but limited conception. One thinks of roads and police, public health and elementary schools. It means under Communism the entire organization of life. The State is manufacturer and merchant, farmer and railway director, and on the brains at its head, and the bureaucratic machinery below them, every detail of the citizen's welfare depends. The work of every counting-house and bank has been concentrated in the buildings which the administration occupies at intervals all along the straggling main street of Vladímir. The clerks, and all but the directing officials, are in the main the same people who conducted the business of Vladímir in the old days. The banker's cashier and the merchant's book-keeper have now become civil servants. The young women who would have been typing and calculating in a hundred separate offices are now working at rather similar tasks in a few big rooms. So far as mere machinery goes, much the same change would have taken place if a few big Trusts had amalgamated and centralized all the textile, metallurgical, transport and agricul-

tural business of the province. Nearly everyone
in what we call the " middle class " (Russians with
more dignity describe it as the " intelligentsia ")
is now a public servant on salary and rations. Only
the big capitalists and landlords have fled. A very
few of the formerly rich still exist in idleness, living
rather mysteriously—as they say themselves, by
selling what is left of their former luxury, or, as the
Communists suspect, by taking a hand in illicit trade.

The analogy of the few big Trusts is only partly
applicable. The Soviet economy produces for use
and not for profit. Finance has almost lost its
meaning. A Communist State is solvent if it can
get from the land food to supply its industrial workers,
and from its industrial workers goods to satisfy its
peasants. It will do well if, when this equation is
satisfied, it can also, with a surplus of food and
clothing, employ teachers, artists, musicians and
builders for the common good. It will thrive if it can
also find a surplus of food and clothing sufficient to
permit it to divert labour to " capital " undertakings
—the making of great electric power stations, for
example. It must, for some of its needs, trade
with foreign lands ; and here again its problem is
simply to feed and clothe a given number of peasants
or miners, who will produce a surplus of something
exportable. Its entire problem, in short, is a labour
problem. That, one may remark, is everywhere
the root fact. But in Soviet Russia the problem is
reduced to its essentials. The complications of
finance, profit and marketing are eliminated. The
difficulty with which Soviet Russia wrestles to-day
is at bottom a labour difficulty. It must waste
millions of workers on its armies. It has lost millions
of industrial workers, because they have gone back

from the factory to the land, which now belongs to them, or because they now find whole-time instead of the former part-time employment on their enlarged holdings. It has to watch the waste (in effect) of other millions of workers, because the peasants cannot cultivate even with moderate efficiency. To solve this labour problem is the central object of Soviet administration in Vladímir as elsewhere.

Of some of the men at the head of the Soviet administration I saw a good deal, and on the whole my impression was favourable. All of them, except the Directors of Education and Health, had been manual workers, and all except the Director of Health were Communists. I heard them described by hostile " intellectuals " as mere " Izvóstchiks " (cab-drivers) and " unlettered labourers." Such phrases, I think, expressed only the contempt of the vulgar middle-class mind for the man who works with his hands, and I heard them more often from half-educated persons than from doctors or teachers, who often spoke well of the administration. President Kudráshev, who liked to encourage my limping Russian, was a man of dignified presence and courteous speech, who made an admirable chairman of the Soviet. I once heard him quote a Russian classic in a way that showed familiarity, and the clear and connected account which he gave me of the history of Vladímir since the Revolution could have come only from a disciplined mind. With another colleague, one of the three heads of the Department of Production, I spent a whole day. An engineer by trade, he delighted me by his lucid disquisitions on machinery, in which he showed no mean knowledge of theoretical mechanics and mathematics. He reminded me of a Scotch carpenter, known to me in boyhood, who became a teacher of science. He was the typical Communist, idealist yet realist, his brain on fire with schemes for turning science to account to develop the neglected resources of Russia. I got him to talk freely about the " intellectuals " who served under him. On some of them, chiefly architects and engineers, he poured the most generous eulogy. They were, he said, men with the spirit of " artists," who worked for the pleasure of creation and the motive of service. He paid a high tribute to their zeal, and said they would often work voluntarily for fourteen or sixteen hours a day. These were always the ablest men of their professions, and with these it was a pleasure to work. Others, the type of man who had only worked for profits and fees in the old days, performed their minimum tasks indifferently. The Director of Education, Comrade Plaksya, was the only University man in the team, plainly an idealist of the self-sacrificing Russian type, gentle, kindly, and in love with his children and his work. The others impressed me less, perhaps because they were more reserved, but they were modest, and frank in speaking of their failures and difficulties—probably, as everyone told me, the abler men were mostly at the front. One could not say, as yet, that the administration attained, by Western standards, a high standard of competence. What Russian administration ever did ? Hard work and courage were its great virtues.

The " Extraordinary Commission " which combats " Counter-Revolution " enjoys a terrible reputation abroad, and in Moscow it certainly is a ruthless engine of terror. If one would form a picture of Russian life, however, one must bear in mind that the vast mass of the Russian population lives in the provinces. There has never been a "terror" in Vladímir, though undoubtedly life had been made harder at one time for the middle class than it is now. The hostile "intellectuals" with whom I talked, guessed that about forty persons had been executed in the whole province since the Revolution, out of a population of 1,600,000. In fact, as the books of the Commission showed, there had been in all seventy-nine persons executed since the Revolution. Of these, according to the records, eighteen had taken part in armed mutinies and were taken with arms; twelve were officials guilty of grave dereliction of duty, usually corruption; twelve were brigands or robbers; twelve were members of the old Tsarist secret police, and twenty-five were military deserters. No one, in short, was shot merely for hostile political opinions. The Commission ceased in February of this year to have the right to pass capital sentences. I looked over the calendar of its less serious cases, which included peculation, bribery, drunkenness and robbery, and found in it only one category of obviously political offences, under the heading "counter-revolutionary and anti-Soviet activities." There were six such cases this year. All but one were acquitted, and this one, sentenced to six months' imprisonment, was released after two months. I heard frequent complaints, which certainly were or had been well founded, of the dilatory procedure of the Extraordinary Commission. Men were often arrested, and "sat," as Russians say, for weeks in prison before a charge was formulated: the prison, moreover, was dirty and the food bad and insufficient. The president admitted the truth of this complaint in the past, but declared that since his own recent appointment, no prisoner had been kept for more than twenty-four hours without a charge. Nothing can alter the fact that this Commission is a summary court, armed until lately with absolute powers, working in secret and admitting no defence save such as the prisoner can make unaided, but its actual record was much milder than its reputation. Its chief work, however, is to act as an examining body which prepares cases for other tribunals. The "Revolutionary Tribunal" is, on the other hand, a regular court, sitting in public, and admitting defence by advocates under the usual forms. I heard nothing to its discredit in Vladímir, and its president impressed me favourably. It has this year (up to the end of September) passed only three capital sentences. Of these cases one was an official, a Communist, who stole Government stores, another, an ex-Tsarist *agent provocateur*, and the third, a deserter from the Army who had twice repeated his offence. In the early stages of the Revolution there certainly was, even in Vladímir, some mean and petty persecution of the middle class. This has admittedly ceased, and even to some of the most quoted cases there were sometimes two sides. I shared, for example, the indignation of some middle-class women when they told me of their worst experience. They had been obliged to scrub dirty barracks last year, and maintained that this was wantonly enforced, solely to humiliate them. Later, from a doctor, I accidentally heard the explanation. It happened after the typhus epidemic, when the victims were so numerous that they were buried in a common grave. All the unoccupied women of Vladímir were "mobilized," without distinction of class, for a drastic cleaning and disinfection of the whole town. One does not see why women, even of gentle birth, should shirk their part in fighting a common peril. If the work assigned was, as in this case, unpleasant and beyond their strength, one may fairly assume some malice on one side, but there was also a lack of public spirit on the other. The Revolution has established absolute sex equality in Russia, but this means that while every office and opportunity is open to women, public service is also expected from them. The root of the difficulty in these cases was that these unhappy women had been brought up to consider all work " unladylike," and nothing would have induced them to volunteer for the kind of work which their education should have fitted them to perform. I found myself pitying them, as I pitied no one else in Russia. They stood daintily and sadly on the fringe of life. Its luxuries and gaieties for them were gone, and they dare not face its duties and adventures. They could no longer find domestic servants, and lived in a round of petty cares. " We no longer think of anything but food," said one of them to me, " not even of Russia. Life has become utterly selfish : it is each for herself and no one helps another." But I met women as well born as these, and better educated, who found life fuller of meaning and joy than ever, as they worked for the children in the Soviet schools and kindergartens. Nor were they absorbed in material cares. They got their " academic " ration and were spared the degradation of running about to hunt for smuggled food. But assuredly Russia is a hard place to-day for those who will not work. It is often hard for those who will, but to them at least life has a meaning.

I should weary the reader if I attempted to reproduce the big dossier of facts and statistics which I collected about the Vladímir administration. On its constructive side, the Agricultural Department was perhaps the most interesting. The land, of course, had been nationalized, but in fact the individual peasant cultivator retains his old holding, and has usually had it enlarged. Though he enjoys no legal property in it, he is in practice left undisturbed and hands it down to his son. He may not sell it or mortgage it, and can in theory be dispossessed if he neglects to cultivate it. The system is, however, for all practical purposes peasant ownership. The landed gentry almost always fled abroad. The problem for the administration is the nearly desperate one of getting a higher yield from an uneconomic system, worked by conservative and illiterate peasants. One has only to see the long, narrow strips of tillage and fallow, rye alternating with thistles, to realize that the first step is to educate the peasant out of his individualism. Some progress has been made. In many villages the peasants are now forming " artéls " (co-operative groups) for common cultivation. The long, narrow strips, a few yards wide, disappear. The separate holdings are amalgamated into big fields. Instead of the alternate tillage and fallow, one sees a six or eight field system, with a proper rotation of crops. For the first time machinery is being used, scarce though it is. Eight tractors belonging to the Department were used for the first time this season. Some hundred and fifty-six villages in this province have adopted the " artél " system since the Revolution.

There are also some " communal " farms, in which the workers not merely produce but also consume in common. They usually live in the big manor house, abandoned by the former proprietor, and have a common kitchen and common meals, while each family has its own room or rooms. This system does not attract the peasants, and is chiefly favoured by industrial Communist workmen returning to the land. I saw one of these farms. The cultivation was immensely better than that of the individual peasants, though the soil was mere sand, and four in seven of the able-bodied men were at the front. The women told me that, thanks to the common kitchen, their domestic work had been halved. The spirit of this commune was certainly one of pride in its work, though it had started under very unfavourable conditions. It had already introduced (it had only existed a year) several crops which the villagers had never before seen in their lives. Its livestock was well cared for, and it had done best with those crops (notably tobacco) which need most attention. One pleasing feature of this colony was the presence in it of two old men, too feeble to work. They shared in the common property and were great favourites with the numerous children. I heard a Communist driving home the moral as he talked to a group of individualist peasants. "What will you do," he asked, "when your black day comes? Join a commune now, and when you are old or ill, the rest of us will work for you." The Communists are deeply attached to the ideal side of this experiment, and see in it the perfect form of social life and work. Two of the working men on this farm were obviously men of more than average intelligence, and one of them broke into real eloquence as he enlarged on the moral beauty of their undertaking. The women, I gathered, were much less contented, in spite of the halving of their domestic work, of which they spoke spontaneously. The difficulty was the usual one in all these experiments. Quarrels are rather frequent, which only means that the human nervous system demands more solitude and more relief from the friction of intercourse than it can get in a commune. I doubt, however, whether these experiments (there are forty-seven in Vladímir province) are quantitatively of much importance or have much future.

More important are the big farms (fifty-eight) managed directly by the Soviet. On these the workers are employees, working for payment in kind and money. They have, of course, their farm "councils," which they value, and they have undoubtedly gained immeasurably by the Revolution, and know it. I had an unusually unembarrassed talk, without an interpreter, with two peasants on one of these farms. Both were rather ragged, but their mood was one of satisfaction. I asked the elder of the two whether things were better or worse since the Revolution. He gave me the last answer that I expected. "Better," he replied very decidedly, "for now we can say what we like. There's no one to be afraid of." I felt startled, for few associate the idea of free speech with the present regime. Some anecdotes about the late proprietor taught me what the old man meant. In the old days he used to make his obeisance and say "Aye, aye, sir," cap in hand, to those above him. Now he spoke his mind to all and called the manager "comrade." Perhaps, in the long run, this form of freedom of speech matters more to the millions than the liberty to circulate critical pamphlets, though it seems well to have both.

The restraints upon the freedom to oppose politically affect a very few. The gain in daily freedom to men who used to bend to a class yoke, affects the multitude. I tried the same simple question with a younger man. He was more expansive, but the result was much the same. " Well," he answered, " I've seen a good deal in my life. I've travelled and knocked about the world. These are hard times. I've seen better and I've seen worse. But we have one great thing that we never had before. We have a farm council. If the manager does any wrong to us *or the farm*, we can discuss it with him, and if he doesn't give way, we can take our complaint in to Vladímir." And that also means freedom. On another of these big estates I saw the social change from another angle. The proprietor had made his money as a manufacturer, and though he was not a harsh man, he had the naïve vanity of the newly rich, who ape feudal manners. Whenever he arrived at the manor house or left it, all the peasants were required to assemble, to take their stand in files along the road, and to make a deep obeisance as he passed. He had one eccentric taste, which was amateur dentistry, and the peasants were obliged to submit themselves to him while he practised ; but for these unpleasant hours there was usually some reward in money. Finally, this personage was a passionate sportsman. " He had forty gamekeepers and one cow," as a peasant put it. Now there are eight cows and a very creditable dairy. An estate that formerly ministered only to a rich man's pleasure now produces, in addition to timber and the usual crops, an ample yield of fruit, vegetables and honey, which are sent as comforts to the Red Army hospitals. Better still, the expert gardeners and dairymen are teaching agriculture to the neighbouring villages, introducing new crops, lending out machines to the peasants, and lecturing even farther afield, while in winter they conduct an adult school.

In the three specimens that I saw, the estate had been visibly improved since the Revolution. New buildings had been constructed, the stock increased and neglected land brought under cultivation. The third of these Soviet farms (which was in the Moscow, not the Vladímir government) interested me because neither the manager nor anyone on the staff was a Communist, and two or three of them were dispossessed gentry from distant places. They were all living very comfortably. There was a pleasant club-room, in which the whole big staff used to assemble for musical evenings. The manager was, as it happened, the chief expert on horse-breeding in the Republic. This farm had always been noted for its trotting-horses, and must always have been well conducted, but since the Revolution it had expanded considerably. It now had fifty horses instead of twenty-five, had brought much waste land under cultivation, doubled its production of rye and tripled its acreage under potatoes and vegetables, besides building a smithy, a carpenter's shop and some workmen's houses, and increasing its beehives (all home-made) from three to twenty. This had been done with less than a proportionate increase of hands, for the working staff had risen only from twenty-five to forty-five. The beautiful animals were shown to me with much pride, and I saw a trotting match. The educated men on this farm also were doing their part in conducting technical courses in agriculture for the neighbouring peasants, and for the first time were lending out stallions to improve the local breed of horses. The manager talked in a somewhat autocratic way about labour problems and (quite properly) the whole technical management of the farm was in his capable hands. But the estate is none the less a workers' republic. Admission to or dismissal from the farm depends on a vote of the entire staff, in each case with a month's probation or notice. At the trotting match (it was Sunday afternoon) the women of the farm came out to watch and sat together. They talked very amicably together and they were all comfortably, if simply, dressed. One was the wife of the former proprietor, another the wife of the trainer, and the third and fourth the wife and daughter of ordinary labourers. That, as a Russian friend who was with me (a non-Communist) remarked, with strict objectivity, was "a social phenomenon which one could not have witnessed before the Revolution."

In attacking the biggest of its labour problems the Vladímir administration was evidently working steadily and well. The original rush of industrial workers and seasonal workers back to the land, which inevitably occurred in the early phases of the Revolution, when the land was given "to the people," was disastrous to industry, nor was its effect to increase the production of food, but rather the contrary. This catastrophe will be remedied only by a gradual movement away from individualism and towards collective production in agriculture. A peasant holding generally yields from five to seven fold of the seed sown ; an "artél" gets from ten to twelve fold, while the better Soviet farms, with expert direction, make twentyfold. Every device of propaganda and education is at work to improve cultivation. The Soviet keeps a big staff of experts to direct and teach the peasants, and has established both short courses of lectures and full-time schools for their technical instruction. It has organized the lending of machinery and of livestock for breeding, but three years, under incessant war and blockade, is a short time in which to measure results.

The officials responsible for industry gave me a frank and melancholy survey. The Vladímir province works in metals, textiles, leather and wood. Of its factories and workshops only two in every five are working at all, though these are usually the biggest and best equipped. Industry has been concentrated, and if there is a big leaven of active Communists in the surviving factories, they now work relatively well. Raw material, owing to the civil war, came irregularly, and much of the machinery was worn out. The output, however, was not negligible. Thus, 4,000 ploughs, 25,000 scythes, about 300,000 sickles, with a number of thrashing-machines, winnowing-fans, and peat-presses had been made during the first half of 1920, and all of these things, except the sickles, were being made for the first time in this province. The rest of the output for the same period included 30,000 spades, 12,500 cooking-stoves, and a miscellaneous assortment of pots and pans and carpenters' tools.

Individual management is now the rule, though the Works Council survives. The discipline of work seems now to be normal, and the cotton-mills (though often stopped for want of cotton) have again reached the pre-war level of production for each machine (70 arshins, i.e. 54 yards daily). The programme laid down in advance was always

5

realized for the Army : it was the civil production which suffered. Thus the Army this year
received 98 per cent. of the boots ordered for
it, while only 40 per cent. of the boots destined for the civil population could be completed. The saw-mills are now near ruin, for
lack of new saws, and realized only 27 per cent.
of the official programme. Grave as the case of
Russian industry is, some parts of Central Europe
are little better. The German textile output was
in 1919 one-third of pre-war figures, and in Austria
the general output of all industries is less than
one-fourth of what it was. The great difference
between the two cases is that while the towns
of Central Europe are full of multitudes of unemployed and half-employed men, every industry
in Russia is lamed for lack of labour.[1]

With the medical staff of the Department of
Health I had a memorable talk. Only one doctor
in the whole province was a Communist, and he
was not in a responsible position. On the other
hand, not one single doctor had fled in the general
exodus of the wealthy class. Every man and woman
had stuck to his post, and few of them seemed interested in politics. One-half had been mobilized
and were at the front ; there remained one hundred
and sixty-five, but no less than thirty had given their
lives in their battle with last year's typhus epidemic.
All medical service is free, and the doctors live like
any other skilled workers of the highest category,
drawing rations on the Red Army scale and earning
from 4,000 to 8,000 roubles monthly. The blockade
has fallen with inhuman cruelty upon the sick, for

[1] A Note at the end of the chapter attempts a summary
statistical survey of the present state of Russian industry.

Russia had never manufactured either drugs or medical instruments. Some have been bought since April, when the blockade was somewhat relaxed, but these went to the wounded, and did not suffice even for their needs. In Vladímir there were no anæsthetics, no caffein (the only medicine of much use in typhus) and little quinine. There was a shortage of every sort of drug, disinfectant and instrument, including even clinical thermometers, though an attempt is now being made to manufacture them in Moscow. Worst of all, perhaps, was the almost total lack of soap.

None the less, the Department of Health had gone to work with courage, intelligence and the Russian talent for improvisation. In spite of the blockade, it had a notable record of constructive achievement. It had set up fifty delousing and disinfecting stations against typhus, and there was, in consequence, no epidemic last winter. It had got typhoid down below the pre-war average. It had opened four new sanatoria for tuberculosis. It had created thirty new dental clinics with free treatment. It had organized perambulating lectures for the villages on hygiene and the care of children and the sick, and was using the cinema for the same purpose. These doctors told me that open prostitution had wholly disappeared since the Revolution, and they attributed a decline in insanity to the prohibition of alcohol. It needs a mental effort to realize that no work for public health, save on the smallest scale, was possible in Russia before the Revolution.

I had gathered all the statistics I wanted and there were now four of the staff in the room, and they began to talk freely. Doctors as a whole were happy, they insisted, because they were devoted to their work and felt that they could " serve their idea." They were " realizing the dreams of a lifetime," which had seemed visionary hitherto. So long as they felt that the Soviet was " working for civilization and health " they would serve it loyally, though none of them were Communists (here one of them repeated much the same thing in German, to make sure that I had understood). Under the old regime they had met with continual obstacles, but now they received every possible encouragement. As he shook hands at parting, the Director said emphatically, " I have never asked the Soviet Government in vain for anything whatever." These were the " intellectuals " described by my friend the engineer who are " artists " and workers. In Soviet Russia it is the idlers and the mercenaries among the intellectuals who are unhappy.

NOTE

The State of Russian Industry.

By studying a particular province one may sample a specimen of Russian life, but the results must be completed by some general survey. Here, however, one has to rely entirely on official statistics. These must be analysed with due caution. One able economist and statistician, Comrade Larin, whose published material I have used freely, is engaged in perpetual controversy with official optimists, and his figures, I should say, are probably rather worse than the actual facts.

There are two necessary standards of comparison. When one compares the figures of output for 1920 with those for 1914, one derives an impression of catastrophic ruin. On the other hand, the comparison of the later with the earlier period of the Revolution often corrects this impression and reveals a rapid improvement. A good deal of constructive work is being done in some departments, which should bear fruit as time goes on.

1. *Fuel.*

The output of coal for the first half of 1920 is only 20 per cent. of the peace yield.

The inferior coal of the Moscow field, which was, till lately, the only coal available, has been developed with some energy. A new electric power station has been constructed and a second is nearly ready. Many new shafts have been sunk, the pumps have been electrified and some short railway lines built. Safety lamps, however, are short, and housing is a difficulty. By September 1920 the monthly yield had passed the pre-Revolution maximum and was at the rate of 45 million poods yearly, as against the former highest level of 43. The yield per man was also rising very rapidly.

The Donetz basin, by far the richest, was almost ruined by Deníkin and Makhnó. The low output estimated for 1920 has been greatly exceeded and the daily average has risen steadily, month by month. The number of miners is also growing, and here also the administration is at work on electrification and housing. Trotsky spent some time lately on the spot and started a big scheme of improvements, beginning with the food and clothing of the men. While an output of only 40 million poods was estimated for 1920, the estimate made by the miners themselves for 1921 is 450 millions.

The Cheliabinsk mines in the Urals were recovered only at the end of 1919. None the less, 28 million poods were realized during 1920, as against a pre-revolutionary $6\frac{1}{2}$ millions. The estimate for 1921 is 50 millions.

The Siberian mines show in 1920 a great increase over 1919 ; the programme was exceeded and 36 millions won in eight months.

In short, the Soviet Government hopes for an immensely better yield next year, and even the figures for the second half of 1920 should be much higher than those for the first half.

The petroleum yield for the first half of 1920 was 33 per cent. of the pre-war figure.

The wood cut for fuel in 1920 was exactly double the supply of 1919.

Peat was also more extensively used, but I have no figures.
In general, the fuel supply for 1920 was double that of the
previous year.

2. Raw Materials.

For cotton, see p. 16.
The area under flax was in 1920 half that of peace-time.
The output of the various kinds of iron ore was respectively
25, 30 and 12 per cent.
The copper output was about half the normal.
Platinum and gold were respectively 33 and 12 per cent.
of the normal.

3. Manufactures.

The actual output of cotton yarn in the first half of 1920
was only a little over 3 per cent. of the normal, and only
250,000 spindles were working.
By November, however, over 500,000 were working, and
at the end of the month about a million.
In view of this rapid improvement, the official estimate
that four millions will be working in 1921 may not be over-
sanguine.   That would give four-fifths of the supply required.
The output of flax yarn was 33 per cent. of the normal.
The woollen-mills (80) worked solely for the Army.   The
only way to increase their output is to arrange for two shifts
at least, but that is difficult in view of the shortage of electric
lamps and of housing for the workers.
The production of iron and steel stood in the first half of
1920 at only 4 per cent. of the normal (due presumably to
the war in the Ukraine) ; rubber (owing obviously to the
blockade) had fallen to 1·7 per cent., and various chemicals
(due probably to the loss of expert workers) to 10 per cent.,
while paper stood at 15 per cent. (due to the wearing out
of the nets) and glass at 18 per cent. of the normal.   The
best figure is tar products (i.e. from burning charcoal), which
is a home industry and yielded 75 per cent. of the normal
output.
These are mainly Larin's figures and are all for the first
half of 1920.

4. Railways.

The decisive figure for the railways is that already given,
which shows that there is now one sound locomotive for

every eight versts of line, as against one to twelve at the beginning of the year and one to three in peace-time.

The absolute increase of locomotives (due to capture and conquest) was from 9,525 to 16,611 between January and August. Of these, 58 or 57 per cent. are always "sick." Industrial traffic increased in this period 75 per cent. The repairing programme marches well, and owing to the rapid improvement between July and October has been speeded up to the extent of 28 per cent. There is available, however, in the workshops only 60 per cent. of the requisite number of workmen, which may explain the disappointing results in the building of new locomotives; but even here there is an improvement (five completed for August, eight for September, out of a monthly standard programme of thirteen).

To sum up : these figures reveal the catastrophic ruin of Russian industry as no words could do, but they also show as clearly the marked tendency to improvement. The " strategical " points are coal, cotton and transport. If the programmes are realized here during 1921, the worst will be over.

My own fear is that the failure of the 1920 harvest may upset all these calculations. If food is scarce for the industrial workers, the estimated output will not be realised. Such news as is available, as this book goes to press, suggests that the expected amount of coal is not being obtained. The gravest risk of all is that seed corn is short, and next year's harvest may therefore be even worse than that of this year.

CHAPTER V

EDUCATION AND ART

THE word "dictatorship," which the Russian Communists use to describe their own monopoly of power in the Socialist State, implies that it will be temporary. It should last, according to the tactical theories of the Revolution, until the capitalist system has wholly disappeared in Russia, until the former privileged ruling class has been absorbed in the general body of citizens, and until the civil war and the external war have ceased. Opponents are sceptical, and doubt whether the moment will ever come when the Communists will voluntarily renounce the power which they have seized. Power intoxicates, and history shows few instances of voluntary abdication, save in the hour of evident failure and defeat.

There is one test to which one may submit a dictatorship which professes to be temporary. Does it educate ? It is difficult to believe in the permanence of any despotism over a well-educated population. Tsardom survived by reason of the abysmal illiteracy of the old Russia, and within certain limits one may make a case for some form of revolutionary dictatorship by pointing to the hopeless ignorance of the peasant masses. The Jesuits, who set up their idyllic

Communist State in Paraguay in the seventeenth
century, taught music, religion, reading and writing to
the gentle Indian population, but they never admitted
them to their own order or shared with them their
own scientific and literary culture. A despotism, be
it brutal or humane, must rest on some obvious
inequality between the rulers and the ruled. In the
modern Class State the forms of democracy are
frustrated not merely by the power of wealth, but
also by the gap in culture between the propertied
and the working classes.

This must be said emphatically for the Russian
Communist Dictatorship, that it is preparing its own
eventual disappearance. It is ripening the whole
Russian people for responsibility and power by its
great work for education. It has striven, amid
inconceivable difficulties, for the prompt enlightenment of the whole nation. It has, moreover, based
its entire system of education, not on any principle
of passivity, receptivity and discipline, but rather
on " self-initiative " and activity. The new generation, which will emerge in a few years from these
modern Russian schools, will have crossed the spiritual
frontier between East and West, and will resemble
the passive, indolent, apathetic Russian of the past
as little as he resembled the average Englishman or
American. As I watched the elder children debating,
questioning and governing themselves, I realized that
by its educational policy alone, the dictatorship has
set a time-limit to its own permanence.

More than a century ago, the French Enlightenment and the Revolution which followed it, gave to
the belief in the efficacy of education its most
ambitious statement. It ignored or denied the
influence of heredity. It preached the infinite malle-

ability of the human mind. It believed that there
was no limit, given suitable conditions, to the " per-
fectibility " of human nature. " In ten years,"
thought Turgot, the whole mentality of the French
nation might be transformed by universal education,
and Condorcet gave to these anticipations their first
statement in a legislative code. If the results in
most European countries have been relatively disappointing, the Socialist would answer that the
experiment of universal education has everywhere
been conducted in the Class State. The privileged
ruling and employing class never seriously intended
that the children of the manual workers should enjoy
the same opportunities as their own. Even advanced
Liberals in contemporary England speak of their
ideal as " the educational ladder," by which they
mean a system which will help the more capable
and ambitious children of the manual workers to
climb above their class. Whatever a few idealists
may have planned or preached, there is no real
attempt to rear the whole mass of working-class
children in the best culture of their age.[1] To my
mind the most inspiring thing in Russia is that the
Socialist Revolution, instantly and instinctively,
began to realize the ideal of universal education,
which the interests and prejudices of class have
thwarted in the rest of Europe. Every fair-minded

[1] As I write this, it is announced that in the interests of
economy all new expenditure on Mr. Fisher's Education
Act is to be suspended. There comes to my mind a statement of the Director of Education in Vladímir that he had
never been stinted by the Soviet for money. The contrast
is painful between our luxurious country, tightening its
purse to the schoolmaster in the first hour of financial alarm,
and revolutionary Russia, half-naked and half-starved, but
yet spending lavishly upon her schools.

observer has given the Bolsheviks credit for their
prompt efforts to send an illiterate people to school.
Their ambition is much bolder. They intend, from
infancy to adolescence, to make for every Russian
child the conditions, both physical and intellectual,
which will enable its mind to evolve its utmost
capacities. They intend that none of the comforts,
none of the pleasures, none of the stimuli, which
awaken the powers of a child born in Europe in a
cultured middle-class home shall be lacking to the
children of the humblest Russian workers. Their
belief is that by a great and self-sacrificing effort the
entire generation which is coming to maturity in
Russia can be raised to a high level of culture. They
will not at once attain their full ambition. They
are hampered by poverty. They suffer from a dearth
of teachers who share their outlook. Many a long
year will pass before the primitive, isolated Russian
village can absorb more than the bare rudiments of
civilization. But this they have achieved: they
have broken the barriers which class and poverty
had raised against education. I saw near Petrograd
a big boarding-school formerly reserved for the
children of the nobility. To-day about three in four
of its inmates are the children of manual workers.
They were, in their bearing and manners, as refined
as the children whose parents belonged to the " intelligentsia," as eager to study, and as keen to enjoy the
pleasures of art and knowledge to which an admirable
staff of teachers introduced them. They were learning
handicrafts as well as sciences and languages, and
whether they exercise a trade or a profession when
they leave school, they will be cultivated men and
women, capable of disciplined thought and æsthetic
pleasure.

The guiding idea of the Soviet Republic is to give the children a preference in everything, from food and clothing to less tangible goods. The explanation of this deliberate policy is not sentimental. Communism is a Messianic doctrine which lives for the future and acts with long-sighted vision. Its ambition is to base the greatness of the world's first Socialist Republic upon a generation of children who will be mentally and physically the superiors of the men and women of to-day. Russians are as a rule aware, even painfully so, of their inferiority in the world of action to Western peoples. Dostoievsky has a character who spent a long night of talk in proving scientifically the inferiority of the Russian stock, and then proceeded to commit suicide. I encountered that state of mind even among peasants. They would speak of Englishmen and Germans as natural supermen. Once, while I was looking at a really excellent exhibition of village handicrafts, a peasant asked me if I had come in to " spy out the poverty of the land." There is to-day a reaction against this excessive humility, and I saw in Moscow a new comedy which ridiculed it. The modern Russian Communist, when he perceives this inferiority, does not commit suicide : he goes and builds a school. It is a puzzling racial phenomenon to diagnose. Disciples of Montesquieu or Buckle might invent plausible reasons to explain the racial apathy, laziness and passivity. The Communists have their own ready explanation, which has the merit of being inspiring. It is, they say, the fruit of centuries of class oppression, and especially of the brutally stupid land system. The cure for it is, therefore, Socialism. I talked one night in the train with a Red Army officer, a simple but active-minded man, who had

been a baker in civil life. "What can you expect
of us?" he said. "We grew up as slaves. The capitalistic system has ruined us, mind and body. This
generation is hopeless. You will see the greatness
of Russia only when our children grow up, reared
in a socialistic society." That thought penetrates
the whole Revolution.

*   *   *   *   *

If the Communist party were able to realize its
ideal programme of education, all the children of
Russia would be reared away from their homes,
in village colonies or boarding-schools. The aim in
these institutions is to create an atmosphere of
happiness, social duty, freedom and activity, in which
the child shall grow up to the utmost stature of
which he is capable. Though much has been done
to equalize housing conditions in the towns, by
quartering working-class families in " bourgeois "
houses which were too big for the real needs of their
tenants, home conditions are still far from being
satisfactory. Many of the parents are ignorant,
dirty and superstitious. The ideal plan, so runs the
argument, would be to place the children in common
homes, where they will have around them every aid
to knowledge and every stimulus to their æsthetic
perceptions, learn cleanliness, order and habits of
punctual activity, and escape the incubus of superstition. Moreover, since the Communist State aims
at maximum productivity, work is obligatory for
the women, and, in fact, most of the younger married
women are now employed, in the towns at least,
either in factories or in Government offices. The
mother, therefore, cannot give her whole attention
to the child, and will be overworked if she attempts

it. Feminism, in its Communist form, aims at emancipating her from the greater part of her domestic burdens. The daily public dinner and the crèche and kindergarten serve this end. Furthermore, the really consistent advanced Communist will criticize the family itself. It is, after all, an institution which has passed through many phases of evolution, from matriarchy downwards; why should its present form be sacred? It develops the social instincts of the child in a narrow groove. He learns to concentrate his altruism upon his blood relations, and gains within the four walls of the home no sense of his duties towards the general body of his fellow-citizens. His love to this small world in which he grows up is, in fact, only a slightly enlarged egoism, which is often in conflict with his wider social obligations. It would be much better, so runs the argument, that he should learn from his tenderest years to love elders and companions who are not blood relatives. The school home, in which he lives with teachers and fellow scholars who are not related to him, is a better ethical training ground for the after-life of the factory, the farm and the co-operative commonwealth, than any closed and exclusive family group can be.

I am content to state the position, without discussing it: every reader will supply the obvious objections. The lives of many parents would become meaningless, and the affections of many children miserably impoverished, if this Communist plan were to become universal. They do not, of course, intend to impose it by any kind of compulsion. It is, however, one of several cases in which their unhesitating pursuit of an idea, sound in itself, leads them to ignore the most obvious things in human nature. It is, after all, easy to develop a child's wider sympathies and to create in him a conception of social duty in schools which interest and even absorb him, without taking him out of the home. Russian Communists, after all, are only doing for working-class children, in obedience to theory, what the English upper class, with its public schools, has always done for its own children in obedience to tradition. One need not suppose that the mass of Russian parents, even in the towns, are converted to this view. The average parent, there as elsewhere, has his fierce possessive instincts, and the peasants make great use of child labour. In practice, however, the very difficulties through which Russia is passing to-day have favoured the Communist scheme. Parents who are hard put to it to warm, clothe and feed their children at home, consent for their sakes to let them go to the State colonies and boarding-schools. There are, moreover, tens of thousands of orphans to be cared for. Without an extensive system of boarding-schools, it will be impossible to carry the education of peasant children beyond a rather low elementary level.

In practice, the Soviet Republic can realize its ideal programme only on a limited scale. It lacks teachers, buildings and material, even if the mass of Russian parents were content to allow their children to be educated in colonies or boarding-schools up to the age of sixteen. The official reckoning is that out of some twenty million children in Soviet Russia, two million are living under the roofs of these institutions. As yet they provide only for town children, but in the case of Petrograd and Moscow include an appreciable fraction of the child population. The most picturesque of them are the " colonies," planted as a rule in forests which begin a few miles beyond the suburban area. I saw two of these, in the Sokólniki Park, outside Moscow, and in Tsarskóe Seló, the Russian Windsor, now known as Dyetskóe Seló (Children's Village), outside Petrograd. In the former the children were housed in the wooden pleasure villas built by Moscow merchants as summer residences in this big park, much of which is unspoiled forest. Many of the villas were assigned to ailing or tuberculous children, and these latter, sleeping more or less in the open even in the winter, make wonderfully rapid cures. Others, however, were inhabited by normal children of all ages and both sexes up to the age of sixteen. Boys and girls live together, and co-education is, indeed, the universal rule in all Russian schools. It was August and holiday time, and the children were obviously as happy as the day was long. The younger children went nearly naked, and were quaintly proud of their healthy brown skins. Their manners and discipline seemed to me good, and what pleased me most was that they showed not a trace of shyness. Their teachers and nurses were obviously on the best of terms with them, affectionate and maternal in their bearing, and they evidently thought of a strange visitor, even a foreigner, as part of a world assumed to be friendly. Of the horrible constraint and fear of the old-fashioned English orphanage and " institution " I saw no trace. The villas were clean and tidy, though simply, even barely, furnished, and the children were learning to be personally clean—a lesson they would never have learned at home. Their gardens and vegetable plots were well kept, and they did most of the housework themselves. I took a meal with the children. The food was good and I should say sufficient, though the milk was only condensed.

The unique thing here, and, indeed, in all the new Russian schools, was the prominence given to æsthetic culture. Every villa had its piano. The children evidently revelled in drawing and painting, and were encouraged to exercise their creative fancy. Some of their portraits, and even more their interpretations of Russian fairy-tales, showed unusual talent. They vied with each other, moreover, in writing verses. Each little colony had its " Soviet," in which the children, with the aid of a teacher, learned to discuss their own affairs. I saw one of these in " session," the girls very solemn and business-like and obviously leading the community, the boys much slower and much more reserved. Minutes were kept punctiliously, and the game was evidently educative. Even in remote Vladímir there were some of these colonies, especially a permanent one for tuberculous children, and a big camp in charge of an enthusiastic young doctor, in which several hundred children of all ages spent the summer under canvas, dividing their time between sports and helpful farm work to assist the peasants.

*   *   *   *   *

The long Russian summer holiday was over before I left, and I saw three big schools at work, in and near Petrograd. All were suffering from the lack of materials, especially paper, steel pens, pencils and school-books. But the skill and enthusiasm of the teachers went far to supply the lack. In one of the three, the head master, whose chief interest was natural science, had got together a most creditable physical laboratory, and nearly all the apparatus had been recently made by the elder pupils themselves. Veteran carpenters' benches and lathes had somehow

6

been commandeered, and even the girls were learning to use them. Bootmaking was also taught. The libraries, chiefly of Russian classics, were in great request, and in the evenings the older pupils conducted a sort of literary *salon*. One of these three schools had a rather ambitious theatre, and occasionally the children performed plays of their own composition, usually dealing with some historical subject. Another had a thriving band, which played for me, really very well, with a lad of fourteen as conductor. I heard some German lessons given, and the teachers had managed, almost without books, to make wonderful progress, with the aid chiefly of the blackboard and of drawings prepared by the children themselves. Hardly a word of Russian was used in the foreign language lessons, and in one of these schools some of the elder children, obviously rather proud of their proficiency, started conversing with me in German as I walked about the corridors. Latin and Greek are virtually abolished. For the elder pupils there were lessons in political economy and psychology as well as history, literature and science. The strain on the teachers must have been terrific, and only the best of them could succeed.

I am inclined to think that the schools I saw must have been above the average, for some of the older teachers whom I saw at Vladímir were near despair. " How can I teach English without English books ? " said one old lady to me, almost in tears, and she fell to cursing our blockade. It can be done, but it requires exceptional talent and resolution. Much of the discontent of the more conservative and less efficient teachers was obviously due to their inability to grasp and apply the radical new methods of education prescribed by Lunatchársky and Pokróvsky. The old

routine, which pumped " knowledge " out of text-
books into passive children, was so much easier than
the new methods of activity, " self-initiative " and
realism.   Thus, I found the elder pupils in some
schools learning arithmetic by working over the
actual statistics, percentages and costings of a
particular factory.   That wants a better and keener
teacher than the old book " examples."   Again,
discipline has been a difficulty.   The Revolution came
too suddenly in the schools, with its innovations of
co-education, its children's councils and its abolition
of all punishments.   The first stage in the " middle "
schools was often chaos and occasionally even scandal.[1]

[1] Gossip is always most active over sexual matters, and
there are widespread myths about the effects of co-education
in Russia.   I believe some serious scandals did occur at
first, especially in one Moscow " middle " school.   They
nowhere happened where the teachers retained, and deserved
to retain, their influence.   But in some schools conservative
teachers " sabotaged " in the very early days and made no
attempt to keep discipline.   In the schools which I saw,
the teachers (all non-Communists) said they had found little
difficulty.   Co-education to anyone brought up, as I was, in
a Scotch school where it had been usual, to a certain extent,
for generations, does not   seem   a dangerous innovation.
The statement made recently in the English Press that girls
and boys occupy the same dormitories is a gross untruth.
Every decency is observed.   Some demoralization among
children there is, however, in the Russian towns—much
thieving and some vice.   But it exists on the streets, among
the children who are not at school.   This is general throughout most of Europe to-day, and is the result plainly of
poverty, and probably also of the absence of the father and
the disorganization of the home during four or (in Russia)
six years of war.   German publicists often refer to this fact.
The Czecho-Slovak Minister of Social Welfare wrote recently
of his own country, " The increase in the number of youthful
criminals and of young girls abandoned to prostitution is
terrifying."   The war has literally de-moralized all Europe.

Experience has brought the necessary adaptations. The children's council has now the right only to discuss and suggest, and that under a teacher's guidance, while various " labour " punishments (useful and educative in themselves) have been introduced. The main difficulty now comes in winter in schools in which the children live at home. Many of them are too ill clad and ill shod to venture out of doors, and it sometimes happens that fuel is wholly lacking in the school itself.

The new Russia teems with experiments and innovations in education, and though I saw something of most of them, I have space only for a bare enumeration. There are, for example, preparatory colleges attached to the universities, in which talented workmen (the word, as always in Russia, includes both sexes), nominated by their trade unions, may go through a year's preliminary course to fit them for their higher studies, receiving an allowance and rations the while. The idea is good, but the time in some cases is too short. More novel and even more characteristic is the institution known as the " Proletcult," which exists in Moscow, Petrograd and some other big towns. It aims at developing the artistic gifts of young workmen who have lacked opportunities. It has courses in literature, music, painting and sculpture. I doubt whether much first-rate talent has been discovered. The maturer students have produced a good deal of poetry, some plays and musical compositions, which have been published. These last include some songs of a genuine lyrical quality, along with some deplorable compositions inspired by politics. I heard some of the musical teaching, which was thorough and conscientious, and there were among the students of the opera class in

Petrograd several obviously talented musicians and many voices of good quality. Lastly, it should be mentioned that the Department is working with real enthusiasm for physical culture, hitherto much neglected in Russia. I saw some good gymnastic displays organized by the " Communist Youth," and wondered whether prejudices would soften in England, if it were realized that the Red Army is proud of its football teams. All this, let me remind the reader, has been done by a Government fighting for its life, amid war, civil war and semi-starvation.

How much that is new has actually been achieved in the provinces I tested carefully at Vladímir. The number of elementary schools in the province had risen since the Revolution from 1,793 to 1,910 ; that of " middle " schools from 50 to 62. The number of scholars in the two together had risen from 110,500 to 175,800. There are in this province 317,000 children of school age. The Director of Education apologized for these figures, relatively encouraging as they are. It is useless, as he said, if it were possible, to build new schools until one can equip them. Every child attending school had a right to so many yards of cotton and linen, and his present stock barely sufficed. He had exactly twelve boxes of steel pens for the needs of the whole province. To create a new school is, as he put it, " an heroic act, as difficult as taking a town."

In addition to the ordinary schools, one hundred and forty kindergartens have been opened, of which only one existed before the Revolution. Of these really charming institutions I saw several, and thought them most successful. Everything was scrupulously clean, and the children were genuine Russians in the zest with which they sang long dramatic ballads.

There were also the usual modelling, drawing, plaiting and light musical gymnastics on a new Russian system (Shatsky) which combines Montessori with Froebel. A daily meal was provided for all but the village schools, and in the town even for the children who were not at school. There was, moreover, special provision and extra diet for ailing children, including a big dining-room and playroom for convalescents and a day school and nursery for children threatened with tuberculosis. I saw both and thought them most creditable. Boarding-schools of one sort or another, including orphanages, deaf-and-dumb homes and a new farm colony for moral defectives, had increased from 15 to 78 and contained 3,865 children.

Not the least interesting of the new developments is a Children's Court, composed of a doctor, a teacher and a legal member, which deals with juvenile criminals (chiefly thieves) and has also the right to send children living in a bad moral environment to one of these school homes. It works with a volunteer organization, composed mainly of young people, called " The Brothers and Sisters of Social Aid," which devotes itself to aiding or reclaiming neglected children. Ten of its members from Vladímir are taking a course of instruction in Moscow. The Communists are justly proud of their whole organization for the " protection " (Ochrána) of children— a conception which includes moral welfare, education and recreation as well as the provision of food and hygiene. Several playing-fields for the children have been opened in Vladímir, and there was also a so-called children's " club," in which I saw them doing carpentering, painting and theatricals, voluntarily, but with some help from teachers out of school-hours. In the long summer vacation the children were organized to do such pleasant and useful work as the collection of medicinal herbs and the gathering of fir-cones in the forest for fuel. All this, needless to say, is not only new but unprecedented in Russia.

*   *   *   *   *

The Department of Education is also concerned with the general interests of culture and art, and ministers to adults as well as to children. The Director thought that not more than 25 per cent. of the adult population is still illiterate. In one small industrial town alone—Murom—1,500 illiterate adults took lessons and passed the examination last winter. Before the Revolution, in this province, 20 tea-shops with reading-rooms managed by a temperance society, 50 libraries opened by the Zemstvo, with 2 theatres and 10 cinematographs, exhausted the opportunities for popular education and diversion. There are now, under the Soviet, 58 people's clubs, 677 libraries, 141 village reading-rooms, 884 organized lecture courses or schools for adults, 930 " culture circles " (which read and discuss standard books), 119 theatres, 89 cinematographs and 42 amateur choirs and bands. There are also 11 music schools, 10 art schools and 6 museums, where there were 1, 8 and 1 respectively. The reader must not interpret these words by Western standards. A reading-room is usually a peasant hut adapted for the purpose ; a library may be a room with book-shelves in a mill ; a theatre is usually a wooden shed with benches and a stage, but is sometimes cleverly decorated. These cheap and simple expedients serve their purpose. For the theatre the Russian workmen have developed a passion, and it is by far the most popular medium for the transmission of ideas.

It may be honestly claimed, I think, for the Soviet administration that it has a better record in its relations to art and culture, generally, than any other Government in the civilized world. Let me mention, as one characteristic touch, that in my many wanderings on foot in dilapidated Moscow I noticed only two buildings which had been renovated and repainted : one was the University and the other a workmen's college. Artists, musicians, dancers, authors, actors, professors and scientists do not suffer, save mentally, from the class feud, and all of them who have any recognizable qualification receive rations and salaries—subject, doubtless, to the usual irregularity. Literature, scholarship and science, none the less, have suffered terribly, for the paper shortage is so acute that very few books can be published, and the printers happen to be the most disaffected and the most depressed of all the trades. Poets recite their works in Moscow in clubs and cafés, and the output of new and experimental verse is surprisingly active. Some literary periodicals still appear at irregular intervals, and I read some of this recent poetry. It seemed to me powerful, somewhat violent in expression, realistic, cynical and unhappy in mood, and it was using various new experimental forms. I thought it rather French than Russian in its inspiration, but my slight acquaintance with the language makes my opinion worthless. A good deal of positive intellectual work is still being done, in spite of every difficulty, especially by the scientists, whose researches are encouraged by this impoverished and blockaded Government, in so far as its means permit. I doubt if the crisis in the world of learning is any graver than it is in Germany and Austria, where universities have to cease their publications, learned men occasionally die of hunger and charitable societies distribute old clothes to professors. The Soviet Government has two ambitious publishing schemes in progress. One is a new standard edition of all the Russian classics, which is being printed abroad ; the other is a comprehensive library of translations into Russian from the entire literature of the world.

These books will all go to enrich public libraries. Indeed, the private sale of books has almost ceased, and individuals can buy them only if they require them for their special studies. Given the shortage of books in Russia and the tremendous demand by a newly awakened reading public, this principle is obviously sound. A man who keeps a big private library, in which books may lie undisturbed for years upon the shelves, is certainly behaving in an anti-social way, if others meanwhile are starved of books. But the new system has grave drawbacks. A poet with whom I discussed it lamented the effect on authors. " You publish a book," he said, " and immediately a gulf opens and devours it. You never know what demand readers made for it. It is distributed to the libraries, and that is the last that you hear of it. The old stimulus of appealing to readers who bought your books has gone."

The prospect of not owning books would seem to me personally a serious privation, even if there were a good lending library round the corner. Many Communists talk as though any private possession of any article of consumption were immoral. It struck me that their view of private property had been very loosely thought out. They constantly say, even in books which are intended to have some theoretical value, that the Revolution has abolished private property.   None the less, theft is punished as severely as it is elsewhere.   In fact, and as a rule, everyone retains his private possession of all articles of consumption, subject to the superior right of the State to commandeer them.   What the Communists really mean is, I think, simply that the individual has no absolute rights of property as against the community. He has the ordinarily recognized rights as against other individuals.   His books and his boots are his till the community needs them and takes them. Most Western Socialists would have been content to claim all the means of production for society, without troubling about articles of consumption in actual use. But the dire needs of post-war society drove the Russians farther.   If millions are without boots and the factories cannot make enough, the obvious thing to do is to apply to those who have more boots in their cupboards than they really require.   None the less, it is fairly certain that most people's happiness does depend in some degree on having round them a modest store of things in which their personality can express itself.   If such possessions were forbidden, the mind would suffer from a sort of dumbness, as it does in solitary confinement.

To recur from this digression to the question of books, it seems to me doubtful whether the socialization of publishing can be maintained without grave detriment to the liberty of thought.   A State Publishing House may very well undertake editions of the classics and issue academic and scientific books. But is it, even when, as in Russia, an advisory board of literary men stands behind it, the proper body to select new literature for publication ?   Lenin evidently does not think so, for he has protected the one private publisher who is still active in Soviet Russia against the violent attacks of the Left, which would not pardon his boldness in issuing the memoirs of Victor Tchernóv, the Social Revolutionary leader. Lenin happily ceases to be a doctrinaire when he drops his pen and converses, and Gorky has considerable influence with him.

The painters, who used to work for private patrons, are depressed and indolent for lack of the accustomed encouragement, for there is no one to buy. Some do decorative work for public bodies—sculptors are in some request for the production of statues of Marx and other revolutionary heroes : others earn big fees by doing propagandist cartoons. Painting and the kindred arts depend much more upon the general wealth of a community than music does. If Russia were rich enough to undertake new building, I do not doubt that there would be a tremendous demand for the work of the architects, sculptors and painters, not only for public buildings, but also for the numerous hostels in which public employees are housed, for public kitchens and for schools. A prosperous Communist State would probably be a patron as generous as the Italian cities and churches of the Renaissance. Meanwhile, the public galleries are crowded, and the proletariat is eagerly studying the work of the past. Few people outside Russia realize (I certainly did not) that its pictorial art, in the latter half of the last century, was scarcely inferior to its literature in spirit and originality, and much above it in form and technique. The most noticeable thing about it is, that it reflects as faithfully as the literature, the unrest, the criticism and the irreverence of the Russian intellectuals.

The note of satire, rebellion and bitter pathos in the more popular anecdotal canvases makes a positively comic contrast to our own complacent, sentimental art of the same period. The more recent art is experimenting, and searching self-consciously for new forms and inspirations. Much of it, from echoes of Munich down to repetitions of Picasso, merely copied the West. The October Revolution suddenly inundated the walls of Moscow with posters in all the wilder contemporary manners, including Cubism, and the younger artists had a chance which had never before come to the innovators. They seem to have abused it rashly, for the working men rose in revolt and asked for something which they could understand. The result has been the development of quite a new manner, officially baptized " proletarian art," in the hope that this name may commend it to the people. It is a " primitive " style, which looks extremely simple and straightforward, but in reality displays at its best strong draughtsmanship, with a great sense for movement. I came by chance in Moscow, at the entrance of the Miners' Trade Union Offices, upon some bronze reliefs of miners at work, the strongest and most stimulating thing of its kind that I have seen for many a year. I must confess, however, that very little of the new sculpture pleased me, but I should add that my own attitude to most recent art is unappreciative, which, doubtless, only means that my perceptions are untrained.

The theatre and music, on the other hand, flourish exceedingly. Here the native Russian genius is most at home, and the emancipated proletariat is insatiable in its demands. There is lavish provision for every taste. Companies of trained State artists entertain

the school-children with plays, charades, dancing and
singing. There are propagandist "revolutionary
satires," in rough popular verse, of course socialistic
and anti-clerical, given by touring companies. In
the towns there are in the summer daily open-air
concerts, partly classical, partly popular, with open-
air operas and plays. In Minsk I used to count
three such entertainments going simultaneously.
Vladímir had a recently created choir which sang the
most elaborate music so well that it might have
given concerts with success in London or Paris.
Its orchestra, half military, half amateur, was much
better than any I have ever heard in a small English
town. The opera in Moscow and Petrograd retains
its ancient glory, and there has been no decline in
its standards, though three-fourths of the seats are
allotted at cheap rates to the trade unions. I sat in
the stalls in the glorious Marinsky Theatre listening
to a superb performance of Rimsky-Kórsakov's
Sadkó. Beside me was a group who looked like
London charwomen, rapt and delighted all the time.
"I didn't understand it all," said one, "but I *did*
enjoy it." You may in Moscow enjoy the unique
experience of listening to chamber-music played by
the greatest executants in Russia on a quartet of
Stradivarius instruments. The Revolution brought
them out of their long silence in the glass cases of
rich collectors, "socialized" them and gave them,
like their paintings and their *objets d'art*, to the enjoy-
ment of the world. Judging from the advertised
programme, I could in Moscow have revelled every
evening, had I not been too busy or too tired, in
listening to elaborate music, most of it Russian and
much of it new. Nor does the theatre stand still.
All manner of experiments are in fashion. I visited

one little *salon* theatre, packed with intellectuals, in which a comedy of improvisation was given. The actors invented, or at least professed to invent, the dialogue as they went along. The acting was certainly clever, but I will not pretend that this innovation did more than amuse me—but once more I confess myself a reactionary in art. Though all this experimental art left me personally cold, I mention it to show that art is very much alive.

What struck me most was the universal popularity of music and the theatre. Every club and trade union centre has its own entertainments, sometimes musical, sometimes theatrical. The proletariat is a lavish and exacting Mæcenas. Walking up the Tverskáia in Moscow one warm Sunday evening, when windows and doors were open, I seemed to hear music everywhere. Now it was a brilliant performance of a Chopin nocturne. A little farther on I recognized a familiar theme from one of the later Beethoven string-quartets. Next a choir was singing some unknown Russian chorus, and across the way I watched the crowd streaming in to a play of Andréev's in a trade union club. Sitting one evening at an excellent concert in the former Nobles' Hall at Vladímir, a working man turned to me and said, in his picturesque way, "We used to live in the scullery, and the drawing-room door was shut. We never knew what was behind it. The Revolution broke down the door, and now all this glory is ours." That is one reason why starving Russia endures in patience.

I have tried to describe the least controversial but not the least important work of the Revolution. I will end with a note of criticism. Even here the sharp class feud makes itself felt. The Revolution

does not trust the "intellectuals" even in education,
and retards its own work by recruiting its new
teaching staff far too much from the "reliable"
proletariat (which must first be trained) and far too
little from the suspect "intelligentsia." Thousands
of well-educated men and women are doing routine
work in offices who should be teaching. The old
staff is retained, but it suffers from a depressing
sense of impotence. I recall one talk with a group
of Petrograd teachers who entertained me to tea.
I had seen them at work and admired their zeal and
capacity. A man said first what all were thinking.
There was no freedom of speech or action. It was
like Tsardom, though with a far better and nobler
purpose. He was himself a Socialist, though not
a Communist, and sympathized with the main aims
of the Revolution. But he felt stifled, crushed and
impotent. I turned to a young woman who had
just been explaining to me a new and clever plan of
her own invention for the teaching of arithmetic.
I asked her whether that was also her view.

"It is and it isn't," she answered. "Often I am
very miserable, and wonder if the whole class to which
we belong is doomed to extinction. But that mood
never lasts long. Freedom—yes, we have one kind
of freedom. I am free to work. I love my work.
I love these children, and I am happy while I can
teach them. I know what you will say, Maria
Petrovna" (turning to an elder teacher). "You
will say I am a slave."

"No," said she, evidently touched; "I say you
are a saint."

CHAPTER VI

THE COMMUNIST PARTY

THE Russian Communists have been compared with Plato's guardians, with the French Jacobins, and with the British bureaucracy in India. No analogy can give the faintest conception of the wildness and improbability of this adventure, by which a small minority, mainly composed of manual workers, has brought a vast Empire under an absolute dictatorship and based its rule so securely that every recent visitor to Russia, however hostile, has confessed that no conceivable alternative exists. The world has known aristocracies of race, of wealth, of birth, of talent. Any one of the rival parties in Russia could show a superiority over the Communists in all these particulars. But the Communists surpass their rivals in two respects, first in discipline, and secondly in their courage, their heroic rashness, their unwavering faith, which seems alternately stupid and sublime.

The history of this party under Tsardom goes far to explain its present mentality. Its very existence was a conspiracy. It learned secrecy, suspicion and discipline as the first conditions of success, nay, of survival, in its perpetual struggle with the police.

It had to meet espionage with counter-espionage.
It acquired the habit of unquestioning obedience to
orders, because the safety and even the lives of all
the comrades might depend on the punctuality and
precision of each. No one questioned or criticized
before acting, for prudence required that only the
chiefs should know the plan itself or the reasons for
its adoption. Again and again, in close contact with
the men who are running the bureaucratic machine
of Russia to-day, I was puzzled by some trait of
character, until I recollected that those who are
rulers to-day were hunted conspirators yesterday.
It is this severe training, which taught them to
despise pleasure, to dread drink, to keep a secret,
to obey orders and to live with every sense and
thought alert, which gives them their incontestable
superiority over the idle, pleasure-loving, undisci-
plined upper class which forms the " White " armies.
They were always a party of "no compromise."
They would never collaborate with other revolutionary groups. They used to take a fierce delight
in purging their own ranks of the faint-hearted and
the unorthodox. Lenin's first triumph came when
he deliberately split the Social-Democratic Party
and created the " Bolshevik " (majority) section,
which contained only men on whom he could rely.
These Gideon tactics are characteristic of the man.
In the years of struggle before 1917 he formed a
party which would despise superstition and convention, laugh at danger and forget even the human
ties of comradeship, for the single end of the social
revolution. All the leaders had graduated in prison,
and the Revolution found many of them in Siberia.

Everyone knows that the Russian Communist
party contains only about 600,000 men and women.

Few realize, however, that it is, now more than ever, more careful to keep itself select than to increase its numbers. It is in this respect more like a religious order than any political party which we know in the West. You may enter it only if several members guarantee your reliability, from intimate personal knowledge. Even then you are received not as a member, but only as a "candidate." The novice must submit to regular courses of instruction in the doctrines of the party. He is not received until he passes an examination in the creed. I heard of a recent case in which eight out of twelve candidates were "ploughed" for lack of this theoretic knowledge and sent back to take their schooling over again. Far more severe is the scrutiny of a candidate's conduct. Does he absent himself from party meetings, is he negligent in his public work, is he slow to obey orders? He will not be received. Nor does the scrutiny cease after his admission. Any slackness, any want of zeal, any indiscipline, any conduct inconsistent with Socialist ethics, will entail his expulsion. To drink or play cards would be fatal; even dancing is frowned upon, and there is a tendency to check smoking. The unpardonable sin is any pursuit of gain. I walked once with a young Communist "candidate" through a country market, where everyone was buying and selling in the old, unregenerate "bourgeois" way. He reminded me of Christian in Vanity Fair in his disgust and proud aloofness. At intervals a regular purge, known as a "revision," is carried out in the party, and unworthy members are expelled. It is on record that the doors of the party were once thrown wide open for a week. It was in the black autumn of 1919, when Yudénitch had all but taken Petrograd,

when Deníkin had advanced to Orel, within striking
distance of Moscow, and Poles and Finns might at
any moment set on.   Anyone who joined in that
dark hour must, it was thought, be sincere.   Entry,
it must be added, is always easier for manual
workers than for " intellectuals," and these latter
form an infinitesimal fraction of the party, though
most of the older leaders belong to this suspect class.

The reasons for keeping the party select are as
potent as they ever were.   The Revolution is still
fighting for its life.   When an army wavers, Communist volunteer battalions are thrown into the
breach.   When a regiment lacks steadiness, a stiffen-
ing of Communists is introduced into its ranks.
When a factory works ill, a few Communist workmen are transferred to its staff.   When a village is
disaffected, one or two Communists are sent to live
in it.   They are the leaven, the active, nervous,
conscious element, in the sluggish Russian body.
They are the *élite* of the Revolution, and every man
and woman among them is expected to have will
and magnetism enough to infuse some of his zeal
into others.   If the party were to deteriorate, if it
became less zealous, less self-sacrificing, less audacious, the Revolution itself would collapse.   Another
reason is no less compelling.   It is obvious that a
party which monopolizes power must attract those
whose sole object is to make a career.   That element
the older members, who proved their devotion in
the years of persecution, are sternly resolved to
exclude.

How far do they succeed ?   I put this question
to many people, both adherents and opponents of
the party.   The usual Communist answer ran somewhat thus : We Communists have duties, but no

privileges. We are expected at a moment's notice to obey the commands of the party, and to leave our homes for whatever work is assigned to us, be it organization, administration, fighting or agitation. We are all so overworked that we look on a mobilization order to join the Army as the beginning of a holiday. And yet, if it is to the Army that we are sent, we must face dangers which others escape. The Communist corps are what Germans call "shock troops" and Russians "Battalions of Death." There is no quarter for them in the civil war, and even the Poles shoot every Communist prisoner.[1] The Commissioners in the Army are always shot, if captured, and sometimes tortured first. The "White Guards" have been known to slaughter every Communist whom they could identify among the civilian population when they took a town. If the Revolution should be overthrown, most of us will be massacred. We submit voluntarily to a higher standard of conduct than is imposed upon others. If a Communist officer drinks, if a Communist official steals or takes bribes, he is relentlessly shot, whereas a non-Communist is only imprisoned. Nothing less than strong conviction would induce a man to join our party. Every candidate is discussed and every member watched, and if unworthy motives are suspected, he is at once expelled.

This answer is true so far as it goes. On the other hand, it is obvious that nine Communists in ten enjoy opportunities of power and command which would never come to them under any other regime. That is true of all the workmen, and of the Jews at least among the intellectuals. It is always hard to

[1] This is true. So Polish officers frankly told me in the spring of 1919.

distinguish where ambition begins and a pure zeal for service ends. Most of these men have broken out of cramped lives, which would have brought them little or no opportunity, and now enjoy the widest scope. To some the attraction of the new life may be the importance which they have suddenly attained; to others it is undoubtedly the joy in creative work. Any revolution in Russia which upset the old Tsarist bureaucracy would have brought a new class to power. The " Cadets " are mainly capitalists, shopkeepers and professional men. The " Mensheviks " and the " Social Revolutionaries " are largely intellectuals, who have a following, in the former case of artisans and in the latter of farmers and wealthy peasants. The Communists differ from the other Socialist parties in having a much smaller general staff of intellectuals and a much bigger mass of industrial workers.

The harsher critics of the Communists usually accuse them of abusing their power to make themselves materially comfortable. The charge of luxury is grossly false. Wherever I had a chance of observing them at close quarters (as, for example, at Minsk, during the Peace Conference), the most responsible Bolshevik officials lived in exactly the same way as their typists and clerks. They dress with the utmost simplicity, and the flats in the Kremlin occupied by the People's Commissioners (Cabinet) are merely the chambers of the former officers of the guard. The only elements of partial truth in this accusation are, I think, (1) that everyone, whether Communist or non-Communist, who travels on official business can do so more comfortably than the general public; and (2) that all who do important work, including the Army, the teaching profession and the munition workers, whether they are Communists or not, are rationed on the higher scale. That is essential for efficient administration. One hears much of favouritism in the distribution of clothing and food. One such case on a big scale in the provinces (at Podolsk) was recently exposed by the Soviet inspectors, which means that the party as a whole regarded it as scandalous. Probably there is much more corruption and much more favouritism than is ever exposed. Both were always habitual in Russia. If an opposition Press existed, the gain from its criticism, both in honesty and efficiency, would be immense. One must, however, say for the Communists that they punish detected offenders with terrible severity. Indeed, they probably err here by excess, for if a man's colleagues know that by exposing him they will cause him to be shot, they may spare him, as they would not if the penalty were milder. At present the Communists are certainly not mainly, or even largely, a party of *arrivistes*, and their stern discipline may save them from this blight for some time to come. The severe test will arrive if ever they enjoy ease, prosperity and peace. At present their tendency is rather to a puritanical fanaticism.

With these virile qualities, one must add that the Communist party disdains the mercies and the graces of life. Its journalistic and controversial style is rough and often demagogic. Its intellectual basis is curiously dogmatic, and even Lenin is apt to settle the largest theoretic questions by a simple reference, in the manner of a pedantic theologian, to the authority of Marx or Engels. The general level of ability in the party did not strike me as unusually high, and a gap seemed to separate the bigger men from their immediate lieutenants. If one were to judge Lenin solely by his writings, one would not suppose him to be a great or commanding intellect. He has written nothing that rises above the level of party polemics. The undoubted greatness of the man lies in his temperament—the unending audacity, the buoyancy which no difficulty can disconcert, the daring which applies the doctrines of the study to daily life. He is for ever experimenting, and that on a colossal scale. Rigid and academic though his writing may seem, his mind tests everything afresh in action. He has nothing in common with the narrow pedants and purists of the Left, though his adventurous will may sometimes range him with them, when a daring stroke is under consideration. His irrepressible humour saves him from many follies, but it accounts also for some utterances which come oddly from a powerful statesman. With all his force of will, in spite of his descent from the noble class, he has none of the manners or pretensions of an autocrat, and he spends a great part of his official day in talking with the workmen delegates who come to Moscow from the provinces, or with the simplest Communist " militants " from abroad, listening and questioning all the while. One gathers something of the power of this man's character, which acts on others without the aid of eloquence, from the devotion of his party. Trotsky is, to my thinking, by far the abler writer of the two. His reply to Kautsky is one of the most masterly polemics of our time, and the style (I read it in French) is both polished and pointed. His, I should judge, is the quicker and subtler intellect of these two, but Lenin's is the master will. Popular as Trotsky is, he does not command the same unquestioning devotion as Lenin, nor has he any special following of his own in the party. Tchitchérin, çi-devant aristocrat and ex-diplomatist, is a student who wields a skilful ironic pen, and personally an indefatigable worker, though his strong point, to judge from the state of the Foreign Office, is not organization. Radek, in experience and knowledge, both of books and men, has no equal in his party. Witty, indiscreet, expansive, he is not the least original of these personalities. A foreigner in Russia (he is a Galician Jew) who talks better German or Polish than Russian, with a precarious life of adventure and imprisonment behind him, he incarnates the internationalism of the Revolution. His vivacity and intelligence make him a fascinating talker, and with his quickness there goes an astonishing realism and shrewdness. Krassin, with a German scientific training and the solidity typical of the Siberian pioneer stock, is a powerful force for sobriety and orderly construction. Zinóviev, with more of passion and emotion than the rest, is the recognized leader of the Extremist Left.

Perhaps the oddest trait in the psychology of the Russian Communist party is its combination of ruthlessness with humanitarianism. It has no scruple about sacrificing life. I have heard the leaders talk of the masses of the Red Army as the abundant raw material of victory, very much as Tsarist statesmen used to talk. Few of them feel any compunction for the unnecessary sufferings of the dispossessed, and their ruthlessness towards workmen who strike or neglect their duty is even more remarkable. All this is combined with a humane work for children, for mothers and the sick which puts richer communities to shame. Fanaticism is not the whole explanation. The trait is Russian as well as Communist. One can understand Russians only by repeating daily to oneself the simple historical fact that they escaped the Renaissance, the Reformation and the French " Enlightenment "—all the movements which made our Western tradition of individualism. With us these movements percolated downwards, through church, chapel and platform, even to the uneducated. In Russia they touched only the intellectuals, and that only in the last century. It is often said of Russians that they are half Asiatics, and in their controversies they even say it of themselves. The fact is, rather, that their culture is astonishingly recent. With his own royal hand Peter the Great would cut off the heads of his rebellious archers of the guard in the Red Square in Moscow. There was no university in Russia till the middle of the eighteenth century. The glorious literature dates only from the end of the Napoleonic wars. To all that evolved and deepened our sense of personality and human right, this people was a stranger till yesterday. For good and for evil, Russians count in millions and not in units. Their attitude towards the value or rights of the individual can never be that of the West.

The composition of this audacious party interested me greatly, and I found some illuminating statistics. It is the party of youth. Here, for example, is a classification of the Communist party of Samára town in July 1919, according to age :

16—18 years	..	..	..	67 members
19—30 years	..	..	..	1,353 members
31—40 years	..	..	..	607 members
Over 40 years	..	..	..	205 members

The men numbered 1,912 and the women only 247. Their occupations were as follows :

Manual workers	1,293
Clerks and official employees	489
Peasants	156
Doctors, teachers, etc.	154

The main body of the party in this case consists of male manual workers between twenty and thirty years of age. The proportion of "intellectuals" among the members was, I think, unusually high in Samára, and the proportion of women rather low. Very few peasants actually join the party. Thus, in the province of Ryazan (Central Russia), in November 1919, there were in the towns 3,369 members, but in the country only 938, which meant only 0·4 of the rural population.

Another test is furnished by the statistics of the Sverdlóv University at Moscow, the college in which the new ruling class is training its civil service. Here about a thousand young men and women, drawn from the working class, receive a rapid course of instruction in political science from the Communist standpoint. They study for six months, taking courses in political economy, the history of civilization, Russian history, statistics and the history and doctrines of Marxist Socialism. Thereafter, they specialize in some one department of administration (agriculture, food, education, etc.), and the lectures are followed by practical work in the Ministry which specially interests them. One cannot make experts in six months, and a two years' course will be started this winter. The students seemed alert and full of mental life, and even the shorter course gives them an intellectual stimulus and an invaluable introduction to home reading and private study. This college is only one of the innumerable schools and courses which train young men and women for every imaginable phase of public and social work. The students who are to form the civil service of the new Russia are nominated by the local Soviets, the trade unions, the local Communist organizations or the Army. They represented no less than twenty-five nation-alities, including even the half-civilized Asiatic races, but Great Russians predominated, with 73 per cent., and Jews came next, though they had only 7·5 per cent. The women were less than one in five of the total number, and two-thirds of the students were between the ages of eighteen and twenty-five. The audacity of proletarian rule was revealed in the educational statistics. Seven per cent. had had no schooling at all, and were described as self-taught, while 75 per cent. had had an elementary education only. Exactly half the students had been industrial workers ; the intellectual proletariat (clerks, teachers, etc.) came next, with 31 per cent., while peasants accounted only for 15 per cent.[1] Over nine-tenths of the students were Communists in one degree or another of initiation, while 91 were classed as " non-party," a word which doubtless covers some timid Mensheviks.

The Communist party now recruits itself largely from the youths who are growing up to manhood and womanhood under the Revolution. The " Young

[1] The actual numbers of the chief trade groups were : metal workers, 124 ; carpenters, 47 ; tailors, 50 ; textile workers, 19 ; labourers, 92 ; peasants, 150 ; clerks, 218 ; teachers, 57 ; postal workers, 31 ; miners, 23 ; fishermen, 12 ; electricians, 20.

Communist " organization, conducted entirely by the youths themselves, is, with its 400,000 members, nearly as numerous as the party itself. A deputation of four alert and unembarrassed youths of the Vladímir group called on me one evening, partly to describe their own work and partly to ask me questions about the British Labour movement. They have 9,000 members in Vladímir province (one-third of them girls), while the grown-up party has only 5,850. They arrange courses, at which a lecturer deals, for example, with Karl Marx, and the group thereafter discusses the subject in his absence. They are also active in promoting sports and gymnastics, and I saw later a very good display. They spread their doctrines by organizing " non-party " conferences of young people, at which they propound Socialist theses and open debates. They aim at permeating the schools, and have very definite ideals of education. When I asked for a definition of their aim, one of these youths gave it promptly : " We aim at creating a new psychology of social duty : we want those who enjoy free higher education to learn to devote themselves to society, to repay what the State has given them in the school, and not to be content with a few hours of regulated, perfunctory work." The Vladímir group was helping especially to improve conditions in the orphanages, and some of them worked voluntarily in the kindergartens. They aimed, too, at bringing young peasants and town workers together, organizing excursions in which young factory workers visited farms, and vice versa. They were also trying, mainly by organizing excursions of peasant lads to model and communal farms, to suggest to them the advantages of co-operative agriculture. I asked them how far they were reaching the children of parents hostile to Socialism. They answered that in several cases they had enlisted the children of priests and of " kulaks " (the word means " fists," and is a nick-name for the close-fisted village traders, usurers and rich peasants), and they mentioned lads by name whose fathers had tried in vain to thrash the Communism out of them. With the children of " rich but not intelligent " families (as they quaintly put it) they usually failed. They left their weekly newspaper with me, and in it I found these typical reports of the activities of the " Communist Youth " elsewhere in Russia :

" In a certain village, the ' Communist Youth ' has opened a factory for soap, and is distributing it free, with appeals for cleanliness."

" In another village, a boot-repairing workshop has been opened, to repair, free of charge, the boots of the families of absent soldiers."

" Another : The group has organized itself to fight epi-demics."

" Another : The group has registered all illiterates from sixteen to fifty years of age, and opened a class for them with 150 pupils."

" Kazan : 35 libraries opened ; 1,500 Moslem members enrolled, including 250 girls."

" Another : Collected old iron and made ploughs for the peasants."

" Suzdal (near Vladímir) : The secretary was censured for wasting his time at evening dances."

" Turkestan : Organized a collection for the starving children of Petrograd and Moscow."

These youths were very dogmatic and very sure of themselves, but they will make good citizens, who will help to organize Russia out of the sloth and passivity of centuries.

Even when one reckons their candidates, "sympathizers" and youthful converts, the Russian Communists can hardly number 1,500,000 persons. It seems a slender basis for a dictatorship over 120 millions, of whom about 80 millions are enfranchised adults. The fact of the dictatorship is boldly avowed. Thus Zinóviev, the head of the Petrograd administration, writes in the explanatory report presented to the recent Congress of the Third International:

> Every conscious proletarian in Russia knows that without the iron dictatorship of the Communist party the Soviet Government would not have retained power for three weeks, let alone for three years. . . . The dictatorship of the working class cannot be realized otherwise than by means of the dictatorship of its advanced guard—the Communist party.

The survival of the dictatorship is a much more remarkable fact than its creation. Indeed, one of the ablest leaders told me that in 1917 they hardly hoped to maintain themselves for two months. Their opponents were more inert and more inept than they had realized. There is no doubt that in Central Russia the majority of the population welcomed the Revolution. I was amazed to discover, from a study of the statistics of the elections for the Constituent Assembly, taken on an orthodox democratic basis, that the Bolsheviks had polled a clear 55 per cent. of all the votes cast in Northern and Central Russia, including Moscow, Petrograd and the North-Western and West-Central armies. They were outvoted in the richer outlying parts of Russia, the Ukraine, the South, the Caucasus and Siberia, where the Social Revolutionaries predominated. These regions they have slowly conquered, thanks mainly to the folly and brutality of the " White ":

Generals.   If one asks how the dictatorship has been
maintained, the answer is, partly by unremitting
propaganda, partly by terror, but chiefly by the
adroit seizure of the decisive tactical " positions "—
the Soviets, the trade unions and the Army.

The worst detail of the Russian Soviet system is
that voting is open, and usually by a show of hands,
so that every opponent becomes a marked man.
For the inequality which favours the industrial as
against the backward and illiterate rural areas a
good defence may be made.   The franchise is now
almost universal, for the employing class, originally
excluded, is now absorbed among the salaried
workers, save for the bigger farmers in the rich
agricultural districts.   The Communists contrive to
keep an overwhelming majority in the Soviets,
mainly by repressing the propaganda of their
opponents.   It is broadly true that there is now no
opposition Press in Russia, though the Left Social
Revolutionaries have a monthly organ and the
Jewish parties, not yet wholly absorbed, have several
weekly organs.   The Menshevik leaders told me of
their difficulties.   They can get no paper, which is
a Government monopoly, for pamphlets or leaflets
at election time.   They can rarely hire a hall for
public meetings, though they can and do speak at
the meetings called by the various bodies of electors
(e.g. Soviet employees).   They succeed as a rule
only in factories, where propaganda can be done by
word of mouth.   Even so, on one pretext or another,
their candidates are sometimes disqualified, and
their elected members are occasionally expelled
(e.g. in one case, for refusing to join in the election
of Lenin and Trotsky as honorary presidents of the
Soviets).   They are none the less a tolerated and

legal opposition. Other parties, notably the Right
Social Revolutionaries and the " Cadets " (Liberals),
which openly support the " Whites " in the civil
war, are, of course, not tolerated at all as organized
parties.

The governing bodies of the trade unions have
been gradually captured by the Communists, in
most cases by peaceful means. The fact seems to
be that many of the workmen who formerly belonged
to the Mensheviks or Social Revolutionaries have
gone over to the Communists. Two unions which
had special economic reasons for discontent, the
printers and the chemical workers, were drastically
dealt with this year, and their mainly " Menshevik "
executives dissolved.   The co-operative organization has been taken in hand by similar methods,
and its central governing organization is now domi-
nated by Communists. Both are now, in effect,
official State organizations, which represent the
whole body of citizens, as producers in the one case
and as consumers in the other. In some ways the
Communist reorganization of the trade unions has
been valuable. The task was an easy one, for until
the March Revolution few trade unions existed, save
as fleeting underground creations. Such craft unions
as did exist disappeared, and the entire body of
workers, men and women, was grouped in twenty-
two industrial unions. All grades of workers busied
in the same task are thus united in a single body.
One may, in some cases, question the classification,
but the general idea is indisputably sound. Thus,
doctors, nurses and dispensers form a single union.
At the same time, any special section, e.g. doctors,
may form a professional organization of their own
within the union. The whole handling of the

trade union problem is on lines which recall some of the main ideas of Guild Socialism. The intention, already realized in part, is to devolve upon the trade unions the whole conduct of each industry, and they might, if times were peaceful, gradually drive the machinery of the State, with its People's Commissioners, who are simply what the old world called Ministers, into the background. The ultimate ideal is, in short, that the trade unions, through their elected councils, shall manage the whole business of agriculture, the textile industry, teaching and the rest. This devolution is as yet, however, by no means complete, and the unions are concerned only with the labour side of industry, and not with production as a whole. But in fact these trade unions are merely bureaucratic creations. There was no living tradition to work upon, and the sudden change destroyed the little that there was. Few of the unions really represent or express the mind of the workers, and they are in practice simply outgrowths of the Communist party, which organize labour for the State. They lack any corporate spirit of their own, nor will they acquire one, until the dictatorship is relaxed.

Finally, the Army will, ere long, be officered solely by Communists. The professional officers of the old regime, on whom at first Trotsky had to rely for the creation of the Red Army, have grown with each campaign less indispensable, as men promoted from the ranks were trained in the Red cadet battalions. Entry into the military schools, as Trotsky announced in a recent speech, is now confined exclusively to Communists. That means that so long as the men obey their officers, the Army will be a trustworthy tool of the party. It also

8

means that though the Army may be used for aggressive revolutionary designs upon neighbouring States, it could not conceivably be induced to support a military dictatorship. For all these young proletarian officers party discipline means more than military discipline.

Such democracy as there is in Russia exists within the Communist party, and not outside it. It is a grave mistake to suppose that Lenin rules it as an autocrat. Every new departure in Russian policy, whether internal or external, is debated at the elected Congresses of the party, and its elected Executive is the real controlling power, whose sanction is required even for rapid decisions of State. The inevitable divisions of opinion are often sharply marked in the party and among its leaders. Tchitchérin and Radek are now the ablest moderates, while Zinóviev and Buchárin lead the Left. Lenin balances, and holds the party together. The official Press is by no means tame, and writers of the Left often supply the lack of an opposition. Controversies between leading Communists in the Press are not infrequent. The vote of the party Congress, however, closes all debate, and the minority submits absolutely. Meetings of the party are always held before the sittings of the national and provincial Soviets, and all important decisions are taken in advance, with the result that the party appears in public as a solid block, voting like one man. Discipline so rigid as this, is destructive of representative government and goes far to explain the decay of the Soviets.

With the Soviets, the trade unions, the co-operatives and the Army under its own control, the Communist party commands the whole organized

life of Russia. Behind these open organs of the
dictatorship there works the formidable apparatus of
the "Terror," managed by the Extraordinary Commission. In its early days the dictatorship was
mild. It is true that leading opponents were placed
under preventive arrest, but apart from some murders,
there were at first no authorized executions. The
main business of the Extraordinary Commission was
at first to cope with the anarchy and insecurity
which had been inherited from the Kérensky regime.
It rounded up robbers and brigands, and shot them
ruthlessly. The real political "Terror" began only
in the moment of panic which followed the attempt
to assassinate Lenin in the autumn of 1918. Some
of the more sophisticated Left Wing Communists
consciously wished to repeat the excesses of 1793,
and the conditions of the time—the hostile coalition
of foreign Powers, the alliance between the native
opposition and the external foe, the use of money
by the enemy Powers to foment internal conspiracy
and discontent—all reproduced the atmosphere of
the French Terror. It has never, fortunately,
equalled its model in madness or extent. One must
concede that an efficient political police was necessary to cope with the plots which are inevitable in
any civil war. An insecure Government is driven to
an excessive use of the death penalty, for the simple
reason that imprisonment does not deter, when the
opposition believes that a counter-revolution, which
will release all prisoners, is imminent. One must
strive to understand the conditions which made
the Terror, but nothing can excuse its cruelty. To
save the revolution, it is ruining Russia. The Extraordinary Commission, which, of course, examines its
prisoners but allows no regular, open trial, admits

to shooting 8,500 persons up to May 1920. Without an accurate classification, it is hard to form a judgment on these figures. Most of those executed were captured at or behind the front. Some were military deserters; others were marauders and bandits: some were guilty of peculation and corruption, a terrible crime in a hunger-stricken land; others were spies and active agents of the foreign and domestic enemy in a bitter civil war. It is impossible to guess how many, under the vaguer charges of " speculation " or " counter-revolution," were really the victims of class hatred and partisan intolerance, but the number, whatever it is, is too high. I doubt, however, whether many were executed merely for hostile political opinions. The leaders of the Menshevik party told me that only eleven of their active members had been executed since the beginning of the Revolution. They suffered more severely from sudden capricious arrests than from shootings. There was a " round up " of Mensheviks in Moscow, while I was there, on a scale worthy of Dublin Castle. About seven hundred were imprisoned for no reason that I could ascertain, kept for a few days, and then, with some few exceptions, released. Of the prisons it is perhaps sufficient to say that they remain traditionally Russian. Some are filled with men of honour, chiefly Social Revolutionaries, who in the past served Russia well. The " Terror " should have ended last February, when the Extraordinary Commission was deprived of its power to pass death sentences, but with the Polish offensive, executions began again, and averaged three hundred a month.

Almost worse than the bloodshed is the demoralization caused by this irresponsible tyranny. Its directors have developed the casuistry of all fanatics. All means for them are good which seem to their narrow minds to serve the end, and humanity and truth are consciously disregarded, if the cause of Communism may thereby, on a short view, be served. Communists have a trick of laughing at " bourgeois morality," and though it may be fairly argued that our current ethics have been formed to suit the capitalist system, this argument in the mouths of half-educated men becomes a pretext for disregarding all morality. The Extraordinary Commission, though its operations are mild in the central provinces, has in the great towns poisoned all social life by its over-developed system of espionage. Nor does it scruple to employ the *agent provocateur*. The pervading atmosphere of suspicion penetrates everywhere, and in every group and circle there are persons who are said to be spies of the Extraordinary Commission. I saw much in Moscow of a very brilliant man, an ex-officer and former landowner, who was, moreover, a poet of some note, and had a store of unusual erudition, which made him a most entertaining talker. A lady, also a person of charm and cleverness, warned me very seriously against him as a spy of the terrible Commission. A week later a journalist came to me and warned me against both of them, but more especially against the lady. I imagine that similar comedies were going on in every office, every club and every factory of Moscow. The Commission overshadows all social and civic life and reproduces one of the most odious aspects of Tsardom. By its ugly example it is turning to meanness and ruthlessness multitudes of young men whose natural temper is open and generous. Unless its activities are speedily ended, it will go far to blight the nobler side of Russian Communism. It is crushing civic courage and demoralizing alike those who use it and those who submit to it.

I should give a false impression of Communist tactics if I allowed the reader to suppose that the party relies solely on force. It never scruples to use it. It takes the shortest road to its end. One trifling illustration shows its method. Long before the first Revolution the Academy of Sciences recommended a new orthography. Tsardom did nothing. Then Kérensky came in and "imposed" the new spelling by a decree. Nothing happened and no one obeyed. The Bolsheviks succeeded him, and at once enforced the new system by the simple expedient of sending Red Guards round to all the printing offices to remove the type of the superfluous letters abolished by the Academy. With Kérensky and his school the word was the beginning —and the end. The Bolsheviks are men of action. Yet no Government in the civilized world makes an adroiter use than they of the methods of persuasion, propaganda and education. Rifles are ready in the last resort, but placards are lavishly used to economize powder and shot. The walls of every town are covered with the kind of coloured cartoons, humorous drawings and whimsical rhymes which in England one sees only during elections. Every crisis, every difficulty is used to read the plain man a lesson in economics and geography. He may go short of sugar or cotton or oil, but at least the Soviet Government takes care to explain to him exactly why he goes short. A picture map of Russia shows him precisely how the civil war cuts him off from these things. Even the peasants, who formerly had no conception at all of Russia as a State or as an economic whole, are beginning to grasp its unity. Other posters deal with the transport crisis or the shortage of textiles, and the man in the street learns to watch the successes of the railway repairing shops, much as he follows the march of the Red armies. The result is that the workmen in these shops feel that the eyes of a nation are upon them. Placards illustrate pictorially all the various means of social service which happen at the moment to be most required, from nursing wounded soldiers to clearing the snow from railway tracks, a simple lesson in civic morals, by pictures, which even the illiterate can understand. One placard I saw appealed for the more equal treatment of women, and quoted some unpleasant Russian proverbs as shameful symptoms of the brutality of the past. Others are in a gayer vein and pour satire, often rough, but usually amusing, on the three enemies of the Revolution—the capitalist, the aristocratic soldier and the priest. Every railway station and every provincial town has its " agit punkt," a public reading-room, hung with these cartoons, in which leaflets are distributed and speeches made. I saw these places packed. There are travelling libraries which perambulate all the railways, distributing pamphlets, leaflets and books. There are also the famous propaganda trains, six in number, equipped with every device of publicity—a theatre, a cinematograph, a band, a printing-press and lecturers who can discourse in all the languages of Russia on every topic of the day, from the crimes of Wrangel and Millerand down to the best way of destroying lice. These methods are making life infinitely more interesting than it was. Capitalist society makes the mind of the people by its unorganized quasi-monopoly of the printing-press. The Communists, by their organized monopoly, are steadily and rapidly making the mind of this receptive Russian nation. One example will show the curious combination of persuasion and force. There is an armed gendarmerie, whose business it is to collect the requisitioned grain from the peasants. Tolstoy has described the floggings with which taxes were collected in the old days. The Communist gendarmes start work by holding a meeting, at which expert " agitators " (this word is freely used) play on the feelings of the peasants and paint the dire need of the towns and the Army. Then the gendarmes take off their coats, borrow scythes and help to gather the harvest. Only if they have entirely failed, by eloquence and good offices, to win the peasants, is force used—but then it is used without pity or measure.

I spent a morning at Vladímir in talking to Communist " agitators " (the most interesting and attractive of them were women) whose business it is to work among the peasants. It is hard work to induce the mothers in the villages to trust their children to the new schools. No force is used. Instead, excursions of mothers are organized to see the kindergartens in the towns, and presently appeals come pouring in for the creation of similar institutions in the villages. The " agitators " are never satisfied until they have set the younger and more intelligent women to work on some kind of social service, and they are slowly coming forward now to take training courses as nursing sisters or kindergarten teachers. I saw one of the latter courses at Vladímir, and heard the young women, all peasants or former factory workers, discussing child psychology with real interest and intelligence.

The chief difficulty in the villages is the religious question. There is full religious toleration in Russia, but the Communist party is fiercely anti-clerical, and conducts an unremitting controversy with the Orthodox Church—certainly the most reactionary and the most grossly superstitious form of belief that survives in the civilized world. The attitude of the average Communist to religion was like nothing that I ever met in the West, for nowhere in the West is there a Church so reactionary or so oppressive as the Russian. It is only a few years since the most harmless forms of dissent, a sect of Baptists, for example, were persecuted and repressed. The atheism of the Communists reminded me a little of Shelley's defiant creed, and, indeed, their whole outlook was more like the Anarchist Communism which he imbibed from Godwin, than any contemporary European view of life. In this Russian movement I felt continually a simplicity, a dogmatic confidence, a straightforward rationalism which belong rather to the intellectualism of the eighteenth century than to our own analytic, psychological age. The Russian Church has, so far, survived without difficulty, though it is losing ground with the young. The Moscow churches were usually crowded whenever I entered them, and the wonderful singing suggested no decay in its standards. In vain did the Bolsheviks inscribe " Religion is the people's opiate " upon a wall that faces the shrine of the Iberian Madonna. The people continue, even there, to take the drug. In general, the Revolution has been cautious in its hostility to the Church, and evidently much has been learned from the mistakes of the French Revolution.

In the villages the women and the older peasants

begin by regarding the Communists as "anti-christs," but discussion often wins the young people. It is probably very crude and unenlightened to begin with, but wherever lecturers can be found, the Communists are trying to give the masses some notions of popular science. The failure of the priests to get rain by prayer shook the faith of some villages during this year's drought. Even more shattering to faith was a test to which, in some holy shrines, the Church rashly submitted. It had taught that the bodies of canonized saints remain uncorrupted in their graves until the Resurrection. When the shrines were opened, the saints, of course, turned out to be only mortal dust. The village priests have a bad name for their grasping and acquisitive habits, and they are rarely loved. They are, indeed, little more than customs officers on the frontiers of the next world, who take toll from the anxious travellers. On that evil reputation the Communists play, and combat landlord, "kulak" and priest as the united exploiters of the peasant.

"Every village," said one of these women agitators, "has its own character. A backward village elects old stagers to the Soviet. A progressive village elects youngsters, thinking they are now the rulers. In my village," she went on, "the priest worked hard to carry his own list. The younger people came forward against him with the cry, 'Are you going to vote for the man who used to take your last crust?' He was utterly defeated. Even his sons have come over and are organizing village plays, 'working for the anathema,' as their father says."

This anti-clerical struggle has its ugly side. It was not pleasant to see the young laughing at the old, as they crossed themselves before a specially holy shrine in the main street of Vladímir. Yet any advance in Russia can be purchased only by a sharp breach with the mediæval past. I got a glimpse in these villages of a cleavage so primitive that we of the West can barely with an effort understand it. The Communists are struggling to bridge this gulf between the twentieth century and the twelfth. The Communists stand for rationalism, for an intelligent system of cultivation, for education, and for an active ideal of co-operation and social service, against superstition, waste, illiteracy and passive sloth. This elementary struggle matters, it seems to me, infinitely more in Russia than the controversial issues which divide Mensheviks and other intellectuals from the Communists. Youth is ranged against age in the villages, and the battle is really one between an Oriental conservatism and a modern and Western view of life. Lenin continues the unfinished work of Peter the Great.

CHAPTER VII

AT THE FRONT

MY most vivid recollection of the Red Army is of being surrounded by it. I stood alone on an eminence, and looked down on a serried square of infantrymen with fixed bayonets, with a squadron of cavalry behind them. I resigned myself to the inevitable and did as I was bid. Two battalions of volunteers, with a complement of cavalry and a machine-gun section, had been raised in the province of Vladímir to oppose Baron Wrangel in the Crimea, and their equipment, all of it of local manufacture, had been provided by the trade unions. Their young Colonel (if I may transgress the revolutionary code by using that forbidden word[1]) asked me to tell his men what the British Labour Party was doing to assist them. It was a rather delicate position, for I knew, and these sturdy young men knew, that some of them would meet their death from the aircraft, the tanks and the shells with which Mr. Churchill had equipped their enemy. I found myself facing the ancient cathedral as I mounted the platform, and a sense of the tangled

[1] The proper way to address him is " Comrade Chief of Battalion."

history of our two nations came over me. Seventy
years ago the grandfathers of these men may also
have stood in this square, on their way to face
British guns in the Crimea ; but in those days there
was no International Socialist Movement to make a
sense of comradeship between some of them and
some of us. I told them what our Labour Party
had done to stop the war and end the blockade,
and wished them in its name a victorious and safe
return.

I saw the last parade of these same volunteers on
the day of their departure for the Crimea. Physically
they were a splendid set of men, tall and sturdily
built. Their equipment was excellent—good khaki
cloth, warm overcoats, top-boots and portable tents.
The officers wore uniforms of the same cloth and
cut as the men, and were distinguishable only by the
red badges of rank (stars or squares) on their sleeves.
They were all Communists, all young, and all had
been promoted from the ranks, and had passed
through Trotsky's military school and cadet battalions. The discipline was good and the officers
knew their work and went through it smartly. All
the movements were accurately done and the open-
order skirmishing was excellent. These volunteers
were evidently very much on their mettle and were
smarter than some troops that I had seen at the
Polish front. In Minsk there was less attention to
externals and the men were often untidy, but they
always marched well. The Cossacks affect a dashing
swagger, and the Caucasians in their brilliant uniforms
of red and blue have an eye to style. The " officers "
(I was always corrected when I used this word) are
saluted and wear their badges only on duty. Off
duty they are indistinguishable from the men.

They have a function, but they do not form a caste. They seemed to me on the whole an attractive type, most of them young and keen, adventurous and yet studious. The immense majority are either junior regimental officers of the old Army, who are usually inclined more or less to Socialism, or else Communists promoted from the ranks. I met only two of the rather doubtful aristocratic officers who have rallied to the Revolution. The more typical of them was a çi-devant landowner. He had of course lost his estates, but the peasants had left him his manor house and often brought presents of food. He had served with Yudénitch, but deserted with others in a body after a long debate in which they decided (1) that the self-indulgent White Generals were good for nothing, (2) that the Reds seemed likely to survive, and (3) that the Entente did not really mean to support the Counter-Revolution seriously, but merely gave it help enough to keep the civil war going perpetually, in order, for its own imperialistic reasons, to weaken Russia permanently. This young man was gradually beginning to sympathize with Communist ideas, and he had been much impressed when his wife received, before and after her confinement, the extra mother's ration. The command is now so nearly homogeneous, and so generally imbued with the spirit of the Revolution, that the curious institution of the Civil Commissioners, borrowed from the practice of the French Revolution, who were attached to each battalion to ensure its political reliability, is now retained only for the bigger units and is likely to fall into total disuse.

The Red Army is certainly the most efficient creation of the Revolution. Trotsky has a genius for organization, and he has battled with sharp severity against the slovenly unpunctuality traditional in Russia. His Ministry runs like clockwork, but there is only one other (the Railway Ministry organized by Krassin) which comes near it in precision. I had a brief conversation with him in Moscow. He talks excellent German, and, I am told, equally good French. His manner is quick and decided. He knows exactly the impression he intends to convey, and every word tells. He is a remarkably handsome man, and his whole personality suggests an abounding but disciplined vitality. One feels the "overman," the driving power of an unflinching will, a genius which works upon concrete things by method and order. There is in some of his portraits a slight suggestion of vulgarity. In real life one does not get that impression, and the face seems as refined as the head is powerful. He looked to me rather worn and overstrained, but there was no trace of weariness in his manner. Our talk turned solely on the Polish War, and though it was interesting at the time it is not worth reporting now. I also heard him speak in the Moscow Opera House. The vast audience gave him an enthusiastic ovation. He has an agreeable tenor voice, but his style is somewhat monotonous and his gestures stiff. He enunciates very clearly and rather slowly, so that even I could understand most of what he said. The manner was quiet, and he paced up and down the stage reflectively, choosing his words with care. It was more like a professor's lecture than a demagogue's speech, though the phrasing was vigorous and direct and occasionally sharpened to an epigram. It was the speech of a man who, in spite of his military capacity, still thinks as a politician and an economist.

Strategy and the command are in the hands mainly of two professional soldiers. Colonel Kámenev (to give him his rank in the old Army), the Commander-in-Chief, is, as I heard Radek say, " nearer to us than many who call themselves Communists," and I often heard him compared with Kutúsov, Napoleon's wary and sagacious adversary, so graphically painted in *War and Peace*. Tuchatchévsky, the Chief-of-Staff, who commands at the front, is a more romantic figure. He is only twenty-seven years of age, and was a senior lieutenant when the Revolution took place. He is a Communist, but comes of a noble family, and was a student of music before the war, mainly interested in old violins. As a prisoner in Germany he tried to escape, but his captors were so much intrigued at finding in his room a 'cello which he had made by gluing matches together that they pardoned him. A second escape succeeded, and he rejoined the Army. He took his Staff course and developed a deep interest in military history and the science of strategy. In the early days of the Red Army any officer, especially if he were a Communist, who had science and brains was sure of rapid promotion. It was Tuchatchévsky who commanded against Koltchák and drove him back to Siberia, and his skilful dispositions were also the undoing of Deníkin. I met him at Minsk, a quiet and collected personality, curiously modest and youthful in manner, with the air rather of a student than of a soldier. The really legendary figure of the Red Army is, however, General Budenny (pronounced Boudyónny), a simple sergeant-major of Cossacks in the old Army, and now the dashing cavalry General whose daring rides, usually round the rear of the enemy, have played so great a part in all the Red successes. He is the Marshal Ney of this Revolution, but a rougher and simpler personality, idolized by the whole Army as the type of " proletarian " genius risen from the ranks. He, after all, had some experience as a sergeant, but there are successful Commanders in this Army who before the Revolution had done nothing but bake bread or shave beards.

I can make no guess at the numbers of the Red Army at any given moment : some said it had reached three millions, and it was certainly much over one. A high authority gave me the number of actual combatants engaged in the march on Warsaw and the Corridor as ninety thousand, and he added that for one combatant five or even six men in the rear must be reckoned. Our proportion in France was one to three. The difference is partly explained by the primitive railway system and the relative absence of motor transport ; the whole Army depends on little peasant carts. I was unlucky in missing a chance to see the fighting lines, but one sees something at headquarters. The Army is not a modern force equipped for a trench war, and it is weak in heavy artillery and in aircraft. It is designed for a war of movement, and probably its most effective arm is its cavalry—by no means all Cossack, for quite early in the Revolution, town workmen who had never ridden before were turned into good horsemen. The work of the engineers who repaired the railway which the Poles destroyed in their retreat was both rapid and solid. Discipline is obviously good, and the conduct of the men in the town of Minsk was admirable. Their amusements in Minsk were to attend the numerous theatres, concerts and cinemas, or else to dance in the parks with the blonde White Russian girls. I had never seen a Puritan army before, and was amazed by these young men, officers and soldiers alike, who never drink, never gamble, never riot in taverns, and require none of the hideous provided vice of the West. If the reader asks why the Reds invariably vanquish the Whites, I should give as the first reason that the Reds are sober. I heard several first-hand accounts in Russia of the conduct of " White " troops in captured towns—an orgy of drink, debauchery and robbery, in which the officers led. In the intervals of fighting and work the Red Army becomes something between a school and a political meeting. There are innumerable courses for every grade of intelligence, beginning with reading-lessons for the illiterate. I heard peasants describe their astonishment when a lad who had gone to the front unable to scrawl his own name, began to write quite creditable letters home. Education, as usual, verges into propaganda, and the Army is thoroughly grounded in Marxist principles. In the old Army there was what was quaintly called " literary instruction " : it consisted in learning by heart the rules for saluting various kinds of Generals and Grand Dukes. " In the old days," as Tuchatchévsky put it, " all mention of politics was forbidden : the men were a herd kept down by an aristocratic class. Now every soldier understands why he fights : he fights for ideas familiar to all the workers and for the soil which he possesses. He knows that if he is defeated, all the gains of the Revolution will be lost and that the employers and landlords will return."

* * * * *

Minsk, when I reached it early in August, had

been for a month in the occupation of the Russians and was their General Headquarters. The Poles had left their sign-manual upon it. The railway station and bridges had been burned. There had also been a pogrom, as the Poles went out, which had cost a score of Jewish lives. Some burning had also been done, though on no great scale. The hatred of the whole population for the Poles was intense, and the Orthodox Christians were almost as bitter as the Jews. The Poles, besides maintaining a very brutal secret service, which was said to use torture, for the purpose of combating every species of Socialism, made themselves generally detested by the arrogance of their manners. Their favourite pastime was to cut off the long beards of the orthodox Jews, though some, of a more frugal mind, preferred to supplement their pay by selling licences to the Jews to wear beards.

Communist Russia is tolerant, even indifferent, in all questions of nationality. The little official newspaper was printed every day in Russian, Polish, White Russian and Yiddish. A provisional White Russian Government had been set up, which enjoyed as wide a measure of autonomy as it desired. But this region, after six years of war, is so extensively ruined that it was by no means anxious to stand alone, and counted on Russia to restore its economic life. The White Russian language is little more than a dialect of Russian, and the nationalist sentiment seemed to me very weak—much weaker, for example, than it is in the Ukraine, where there is a relatively numerous middle class.

Communist policy in White Russia was extremely moderate, and aimed only at the very gradual introduction of its system. Experience had brought prudence, and all the members of the provisional administration whom I met insisted on their anxiety to avoid haste. The upper class, including all the big landowners, is Polish, and it fled with the army. The peasants and the Jews both welcomed the Reds, but their motive was rather opposition to the Polish soldiery and landed class than any enthusiasm for Communism. Both, indeed, are individualists to the backbone. The older generation of Jews can imagine no life but that of the petty trader, while the dream of the peasants is to own a small farm of their own. The administration was exceedingly mild, and though a branch of the Extraordinary Commission existed, its only severity was to arrest a few suspects, most of whom were promptly released. No shootings had taken place up to the day of my departure, seven weeks after the occupation began.

The economic policy was equally prudent. No attempt was being made to check private trading and most of the shops were open. Few of the factories were working, but that had been the case also under the Poles. The intention is to nationalize them only very gradually by amalgamating the better equipped concerns. Not more than one-third of the big Polish estates will be run as Soviet farms. The rest of the land was being divided among the peasants for use, but not, of course, for ownership. The chief aim of the administration was to develop the thriving home (kustár) industries, which were famous for the high quality of both woollen and linen cloth which they produced on hand-looms. With these the administration was trying to negotiate so as to organize them co-operatively. It was evidently uphill work. The " kustár " does not want to surrender his right to produce for the open market, and the Government will fail to persuade him to hand over all his wares to the official co-operative societies until it can guarantee him adequate payment in kind, which means primarily in food. That problem, however, has been solved in Central Russia, where " kustár " production is now in some articles the pillar of Soviet economy. It enables the Russian to satisfy his love of village life and his passion for the soil, for most of these men have their patches of land. If Lenin's dream of supplying electric power to the villages can be realized, these home industries may survive permanently.

* * * * *

No region of Europe, except the Northern Departments of France, has suffered a devastation comparable to that which has swept White Russia bare. The process began with the retreat of the Grand Duke Nicholas. He aimed at repeating the strategy of 1812, and Ludendorff, like Napoleon, advanced into a desert. The Orthodox inhabitants, who alone were regarded as genuine Russians, were expected to quit their villages. Over a million were evacuated in overcrowded trains, and those who escaped the starvation and the epidemics were scattered over the Eastern provinces of Russia. Most of the Jews, all the Catholics and a proportion of the Orthodox White Russians remained. The Grand Duke carried with him not only the inhabitants, but as much of the livestock as the peasants failed to hide. Fields went out of cultivation, and when I visited this borderland from the Polish side in the early spring of 1919 I found in some places that the sedentary trading Jews had taken to agriculture, since there was no one else to till the land. By the time the

Germans withdrew, White Russia had lost about 75 per cent. of its horses. That is a ruinous loss, for agriculture and transport both depend mainly on the horse. The Poles in their retreat completed the ruin. The White Russian peasantry had risen in their rear in many districts, and guerrilla bands, in close touch with the Red Army, harassed their communications. Their answer was to burn the villages from which their peasant enemies came. In addition, the retreating army wreaked its anger on unoffending Jewish villages and towns. The Poles suffer from an acute anti-Semitic mania, and a priest whom I met in Minsk during the period of the Polish defeats, ascribed them not at all to the prowess of the Red Army, but solely to the hostility of Jews and Germans. The proof of it was, he said, that the Polish mark fell on the exchange even while the Polish armies were advancing victoriously on Kiev. I wondered a little how he would explain the still more unfortunate plight of the Russian rouble. But Poles never require a reason for attacking Jews. In all, about two-thirds of the villages of White Russia, if I may trust the official statistics of the Provisional Government, had been burned. Nor was this all. The Poles looted before they burned, and they requisitioned the remaining horses of the peasants in order to carry off the booty. The official Russian estimate was that only about one in eight of the pre-war number of horses now remained in White Russia generally. In the county (Uyezd) of Minsk there were 1,600 horses left out of the 9,100 which existed before the war, and this was better than the average. The Polish landlords, who own nearly all the big estates in White Russia, fled with the army, and they carried off not merely their horses and cattle, but sometimes their agricultural machinery as well. In other cases the machines were smashed by the retreating Poles. The Soviet Government was already buying horses for White Russia in Siberia, but they could not arrive in time for the autumn ploughing.

I saw two of these big estates in the county of Minsk. The peasants were in a strange mood of mingled joy and gloom. They felt a fierce delight at the departure of their arrogant Polish masters, but they were near despair when they asked themselves how the land was to be tilled. In one of these estates, which had belonged to Count Chapski, only two out of thirty working horses remained. The cattle also were gone, except a few cows of their own which the peasants had managed to hide. A fine mill, moreover, had been burned by the Polish soldiers. Very little work was being done or could be done, and between elation, despair and uncertainty the peasants were evidently badly demoralized. They had allowed some fields of good tobacco to run to flower and seed for want of a little attention. They wanted to divide the land among themselves, but were deterred from this because of the lack of horses. A neighbouring estate was in a still sadder plight. The fields of beetroot and cabbage were choked with weeds. The manor house stood derelict, and the looters had smashed such fittings as they could not carry off. The byres and stables were empty, and when we asked the peasants why they allowed the crops to go to waste, they answered that they had neither cattle to feed with them, nor horses to carry them to market. The Communists were trying to introduce some order. The grain harvest had been saved by bringing in outside help.

Organizers had been appointed and a scale of rations and wages fixed, but as yet the peasants were gaping helplessly at the catastrophe of the war. The administration has drawn up a sagacious plan of reconstruction, but it was only when I saw these feckless peasants among the ruins, accustomed all their lives to obey, that I realized the tremendous burden of command and responsibility which the Communists have assumed. They must be governors and policemen, landlords and stewards, foremen and clerks, merchants and middlemen all in one.

The peasants will somehow pull themselves together. At the appointed season something stirs in a countryman's blood and he feels that he must plough and sow. I felt less sure about the Jewish population of the towns. In Minsk the old long-bearded traders of the ghetto were selling off their dwindling stores of goods, raising their prices automatically as their stocks decreased. When all is sold, what will they do ? They will smuggle precariously for a time, no doubt, until (as one hopes) the gradual recovery of production fills the official co-operative stores with goods, and drives the speculative trader from the market. The younger and better educated will enter the Soviet bureaucracy. A few, but probably very few, will go out to till the land. The younger leaders of this unhappy race were pondering its future anxiously. The two really living Jewish organizations, the " Bund " and " Poale Zion," are of course Socialist, and rejoiced at the prospect that the Revolution had doomed the unpopular parasitic employments of " the Jewish Street " (as Russians call the ghetto), the petty trade and the usury. They were scheming to start technical education for the masses, so as to create a body of skilled Jewish craftsmen. They hoped also to get some of the Jewish workers upon the land, mixing them with the experienced Christian rural labourers in the Soviet farms. These two parties, though both were rapidly adopting Communist doctrine, were none the less sharply at variance, and " Poale Zion," the more nationalist of the two, said of the " Bund " that it had almost ceased to be a consciously Jewish organization at all. The former party aimed at a sort of political autonomy for the Jews within the Russian Republic, and wished to see separate Jewish Soviets created to manage all the affairs of this " peculiar people," including even their economic and industrial affairs. The " Bund," on the other hand, admitted no distinction between the interests of the Jewish and the Christian proletariats, and asked only for the right to manage the Jewish schools, which is already granted. The bulk of the Jewish population in the Pale is, how-ever, not Socialist at all, and it had not even begun to ask how it should adapt itself to the new con-ditions. An immense emigration to America would thin the ranks of these trading Jews if the road were open, but some talked wistfully of Palestine.

*　　*　　*　　*　　*

I saw one of the big Jewish trading villages which the Poles had burned. Koedánovo, on the main road, twenty-two miles west of Minsk, had about 2,150 Jewish inhabitants. It reminded me of a Bulgarian village in Macedonia after the Turks had dealt with it. It is now a pitiable chaos of rubbish, with a few chimneys and ragged fragments of brick walls standing up amid the cinders. The Orthodox church stood intact, and its bells were ringing gaily for the Mass, as though to celebrate this triumph of the Christian spirit. The synagogues had been burned with the houses and the shops, but not before the Polish soldiers had entered them and sacked them. "Here's for your Moses Trotsky!" said a Polish officer, as he tore up the Book of the Law. One portion of the village, about a third of the whole in extent, had escaped the flames by bribing a Polish officer heavily, but others had taken gifts and then allowed the arson to go on. In these remaining houses the refugees had been quartered. There was more room than one might have supposed, for no one was cumbered with gear. The Poles had taken everything, even the boots and the clothing of the women.

The people, when they discovered that, thanks to some experience in Poland, I could understand their Yiddish-German dialect, crowded round me to tell their story. The pogrom had lasted for three nights and two days (July 10th to 12th). They had seen the preparations long before it began, including the provision of benzine and petrol. They gave the details, with names and amounts, of the bribes paid in vain to the officers, told how the fire-engine had been smashed and of the shots fired on those who tried to carry water in buckets. Eye-witnesses insisted on recounting worse horrors still—violations and murders; but these I will not repeat, for it seems to me that one gives immortality to cruelty by recording it.

I was more concerned to learn something of their actual condition and of their prospects. There was much sickness, and the hospital, which had not been burned, was crowded with typhoid cases. There were no medicines and no milk for the patients.

For the general body of the inhabitants the Soviet administration provided a ration which should have amounted to a pound of bread daily, but had not averaged in fact more than a quarter of a pound. On that they were somehow living, with the addition of a daily bowl of thin soup from a public kitchen. The Government was sending planks and logs to rebuild the houses, but these Jewish shopkeepers, who had passed their sedentary lives behind a counter, wondered helplessly what they would do with the wood when it came. They had never worked with their hands and they had no money to hire labour. By what shifts of trade and smuggling they would contrive to live in a Communist Republic was a still greater puzzle. It was the tragedy of people who had lived softly and now found themselves, without credit or friends, suddenly reduced to the position of possessing nothing save the thin clothes on their backs. One girl, a comely blonde whom I should never have taken for a Jewess, talked better German than the rest, and gradually came forward as their spokeswoman. She had nothing in the world but what she wore. A soldier found her hiding in the fields, and she gave him all her money when he threatened to search her. "I knew what that would mean," as she put it, "for several of the prettier girls were carried off and have never come back." She had prosperous relatives, in particular two brothers, "famous artists," a violinist and a 'cellist, who "give concerts everywhere, even in Vilna and Cracow." But where were they? How could she find them? For herself, she seemed quite helpless. She "could not work," she had "never walked more than a mile in her life." Her little sister was ill, and she could get no milk for her. I asked had she no friends in the neighbouring villages. The simple answer summed up the life-experience of her race: "They are all Christian."

I walked away, seeing against a background of charred walls and heaped cinders a gallery of portraits from this ruined village—the stumbling, gentle, emaciated Rabbi (a most learned man, they said), who had tried to tell of the sufferings of his flock and broke into inarticulate tears; a young man who had seen his mother burned alive; and this pretty, helpless girl, with her pathetic gentility. But in this borderland of tragedy no misery is long unique. As I came to the railway station I saw in front of me a cross. The wood already was rotten and the inscription barely decipherable. It was of a laconic simplicity. "Grave of Refugees" was all it said, with a date that gave the clue. Here was the nameless tomb of some who had fled with the Grand Duke's army. They must have died in the overcrowded train, perhaps of typhus, perhaps of mere starvation. They had been flung out as the train halted at Koedánovo, and this cross recorded their anonymous misery.

I cursed the squalid misery of war. But perhaps I was wrong. These refugees were happy in their deaths. They did not see the Peace.

CHAPTER VIII

THE ARMED DOCTRINE

THERE are two ways of approaching the study of the Russian Revolution. One may treat it as a local phenomenon, which may be isolated and considered as a deeply interesting chapter of Russian history. That, however, involves a false abstraction. One must not ignore the peculiarities, historical, economic and geographical, of Russia's case. Her harsh and negligent despotism, her ability, which has no parallel in Western Europe, to feed herself, even under a blockade, the vast spaces which allow an unstable government to go on consolidating itself even under foreign attack—all these unique conditions go to explain the Revolution and its survival. None the less, the main causes of the Revolution and some of its most characteristic features are common, in one degree or another, to most of Europe. Its primary cause was not so much that inevitable misery of the proletariat which Marx foresaw in the later phases of capitalist society, as a temporary misery due to the collapse and exhaustion of Russia's feeble and artificial industries under the pressure of war and the German blockade.

In varying degrees these conditions—the decay of

industry, the starvation of the urban population and
the moral sickness that follows defeat and despair—
are general throughout Central Europe.   Our capitalist
society, evolving on militarist and imperialist lines,
has by the war and its sequels created the " misery "
which prepares revolution.   It is this ominous uni-
formity in the European scene which forces us to
pay attention to the Russian preaching of a world-
revolution.

*   *   *   *   *

The year 1919 was for Russian internationalism
a period of deliberate and somewhat artificial expan-
sion.   It subsidized and encouraged the Spartacists
of Germany and the Communists of Hungary, and
seemed for a few weeks or months on the verge of
establishing itself in Central Europe.   Failure brought
a certain moderation, and to cite one conspicuous
example, the brilliant, mercurial Karl Radek (one of
the most fascinating talkers I have ever met), who
had volunteered to go out from Moscow to lead the
German Revolution, returned sobered from a German
prison, to lead the extreme Right in the Russian
Communist party.   The triumphant victories of the
Red Army over Koltchák, Yudénitch and Deníkin were
far from begetting a militarist temper.   The troops,
for one thing, were tired.   It was their sixth year
of continuous war.   I met numbers of these young
Communist officers at Minsk, some of them plainly
men of a dashing and adventurous temper, who had
escaped from German war-prisons only to rush into
much graver risks in the civil war; and while all of
them would begin by saying that they were ready
to fight on as long as fight they must, they always
ended by confessing a deadly fatigue and a longing

for a quiet life at home.   The defeat of the " White " Generals had put the Soviet Government in possession of wide provinces, potentially rich but actually devastated.   Wrecked railway-sidings, broken bridges and half-ruined mines called aloud for restoration.   Again, there was at last a breach in the solid phalanx of hostile capitalist States.   Esthonia made peace and opened Reval to trade : there was through this door a gap in the blockade. Mr. Lloyd George initiated negotiations for the resumption of trade, and France was now the only open and irreconcilable enemy.   The result was to cast doubt upon the whole theory on which the Communist party had from the first based its foreign policy.   It had assumed the necessary hostility of the whole capitalist world, reckoned that unremitting efforts would be made to destroy it, and therefore took no pains whatever to be prudent.   If an enemy, it argued, is irreconcilable, you may as well confront him all the while with a defiant challenge.   But here was the British Empire anxious to trade, and even preparing, though somewhat furtively, for peace.

Under these influences, Russia entered in the early months of 1920 an almost idyllic period.   The Army was partly demobilized and partly transformed into labour battalions for reconstructive work.   Munition factories got ready to convert their machinery to peaceful manufacture.   Every provincial Soviet set to work building bridges and schools and started schemes for electrification and the laying of railways. Lenin devoted himself with special zeal to his favourite project for restoring Russian industry by means of electrical power.   The powers of the Extraordinary Commission were curtailed and the Terror ceased.   The railways could devote themselves to civilian traffic, and for a month or two everyone enjoyed a full ration of bread. Best of all, the aloof and negligent intellectuals, who had so far seen chiefly the destructive side of the Revolution, began to rally to it, partly because it looked stable, but even more because they now realized that the Communist party was capable also of construction. In these months Russia felt that she needed peace ; she enjoyed her brief taste of it ; she even deluded herself into believing that it was secure.

The Russian leaders were blind to the Polish danger until it actually broke upon them. A curious chapter of secret history lay behind that confidence. The Poles had never wished well to Deníkin's enterprise, for they dread the possibility of a restored Russian Empire, even more than they dread the Soviet Republic. They had refused to co-operate actively, as French strategists desired, by invading Russia from the West while Deníkin and Yudénitch marched on Moscow and Petrograd. Their passivity at the critical moment was, in fact, the result of an arrangement with Moscow. I met at Minsk Comrade Marchléwski, the leader of the Polish Communists in Russia, a man obviously of much ability and experience, whose dignified and attractive personality made the most favourable impression. He twice visited Poland during 1919 with the object of arranging peace. In July, when he proposed that the Poles should keep the territory they then held, he had been well received, but the answer was, " Your terms are satisfactory, but the Entente will not allow us to make peace." In October, during a visit to Minsk on a Red Cross mission, he succeeded in concluding an informal and secret armistice, which bound both parties to refrain from attack and to observe the lines then held. Moscow hoped to convert this arrangement into a definite peace. It knew Poland's insatiable lust for territory and was prepared to satisfy it.

I need not repeat what is common knowledge, that the Russians tried publicly, between January and March, to convert Marchléwski's informal into a formal armistice and to open peace negotiations with Poland on this basis. That would have involved the sacrifice of a region measuring about 500 by 300 miles, to which the Poles have no just racial claim. To territory as such the Communists feel a sublime indifference, nor do they think in terms of race. Lenin, in making this offer, reckoned on buying a peace which he greatly needed, and the free gift of non-Polish territory which he presented to Poland would only, in his view, be likely to hasten the desired social revolution in Poland. The Poles would be sure to oppress this White Russian population, which sooner or later would revolt. The Poles, however, would not negotiate, for their ambitions had meanwhile become much vaster. They had made terms with their former foe, the Ukrainian guerrilla chief, Petliura, and they proposed to acquire, nominally on his behalf, the whole of the Ukraine up to the Dnieper, including the two cities of Kiev and Odessa. They struck promptly, found the Russians unprepared, and occupied Kiev.

*   *   *   *   *

The Red Army was remobilized once more, and handled with much strategical skill. The war was " popular," in the sense that the whole Russian nation (save only the exiles) was solidly behind the Soviet Government. The Russians have never liked

10

the Poles (one recalls much bitter satire of them in Dostoievsky), but it must be said to the credit of the Communists that they refrained from playing on nationalist passions. All their numerous war-cartoons were aimed not at the Polish nation, but at its grasping governing class. By way of associating even the least Communist sections of the nation with the conduct of the war, General Brussílov and several of the abler ex-Ministers of War of Tsarist times were invited to form an advisory board. It was little more than an ornamental body, for it met only once a fortnight, in Moscow, and concerned itself only with the organization of supplies, and not with strategy.

It is unnecessary to recall in detail the rapid successes of the Red Army over the Poles. By mid-July it had not merely recovered Kiev and driven the Poles out of White Russia; it had even invaded Poland proper. Now came for Moscow a searching political problem. This had been for Russia emphatically a war of defence. She had recovered her territory and taught the invader a salutary lesson. Should she prove her moderation by halting at his frontiers and concluding a clement peace? It takes two to make a reasonable peace, and there was nothing to suggest that the Poles were even now prepared for it. But London intervened, manifestly alarmed by the Red successes and trembling for the consequences in Europe, if a victorious Russian army should sweep onward to the German frontiers. Lord Curzon proposed an equitable frontier for Poland, and offered Allied mediation to arrange a peace. Dialectically it was easy to ridicule this new attitude. For three years the British Government had done its utmost to destroy the

Russian Revolution. Such a Power could not be a neutral mediator, and to go to London would be to admit that Russia had bent to the yoke and acknowledged the sway of the Supreme Council. In a note of that polished irony in which Tchichérin's pen excels, Lord Curzon's offer was politely but decisively rejected.

None the less there was, from a practical standpoint, much to be said for accepting it. Russia was in urgent need of peace. To accept would have hastened the resumption of trade and might have compelled Great Britain to take a decided line of opposition to the French policy of unrelenting war on Russia. There were moderates among the leaders of the Communist party (I heard the inner history of this crisis from one of them) who would have closed with the Curzon offer on one condition—the formal recognition of the Soviet Republic. The Left wing, however, carried the day, and it won because Lenin sided with it.

Let no one suppose that racial antipathy, or greed of territory, or any phase of imperialism whatever, had anything to do with Moscow's decision. Moscow followed one perfectly simple and definite aim, and that was to further the social revolution in Poland. Three reasons influenced it. Firstly, if you are a Communist, you must desire a social revolution everywhere. Secondly, a communized Poland would be in direct touch with Germany and Czecho-Slovakia, and would form a base for propaganda and eventually for armed action, conveniently situated for operations in the whole of Central Europe. Lastly, and this really was the decisive consideration, nothing much less than a social revolution is ever likely to make Poland a good neighbour. The bellicose and romantic

Chauvinism of the Polish landed class has a simple economic root : it owns vast estates in White Russia, Lithuania, Eastern Galicia and the Ukraine, far beyond the Polish border. While this class dominates Poland and leans on the French alliance she is never likely to abandon her immense imperial ambitions. When Lenin argued that security from Polish militarism could be attained only by upsetting this landed caste, he reasoned exactly as President Wilson did when he imposed a democratic revolution on Germany. With all his moderation, Lenin is still a revolutionary; as a shrewd Communist put it, " if he sees even a 20 per cent. chance of success for a revolution he will gamble on it." He believed that if the Red Army showed itself, the Polish workers and the landless peasants would rally to it, and so he decided (in his own phrase) " to test Poland with Russian bayonets." Whether, in cold blood and alone, he would have taken this decision may be doubted. But the moment made for exaltation. Pilgrims from all over Europe, and even from Asia and America, were arriving in Russia for the Congress of the Third International. It was a time of high hopes and excitement, and as these foreign delegates, all optimists, all enthusiasts, made their presence felt, the world-revolution looked imminent to the more visionary Russian Communists. The Left wing clamoured publicly for the continuance of the war till Poland became a Soviet republic, and Lenin aims always at the unity of his party.

The belief that the Poles would rise at the approach of a Russian army exhibits the curious deficiencies of Communist political psychology. Russians, however, know the Poles as little as we Englishmen know the Irish. No race on earth is so fanatically nationalist; and that sentiment is nearly as deeply rooted in the masses as it is in the ruling caste. For them Bolshevism is simply a Russian doctrine, and they see in the Red Army merely a new incarnation of the old forces which oppressed them. A revolution, so long as the war lasted, was a moral impossibility. It might conceivably have happened in the depression of defeat, after a not too rigorous peace. That view was forcibly stated to Lenin by the Polish Communists in Russia, and stated in vain. His Marxist reading of history forbids him to reckon with any but economic motives. The Polish proletariat was in acute penury, therefore it must be ripe for a social revolution. The simpler sort of Communists live in a state of Messianic exaltation, and expect the world-revolution almost from month to month, much as the Jews in the seventeenth century expected the coming of their deliverer. Deep in the Russian soul is a belief in the miraculous, and traces of it survive even in Russians who suppose themselves to be ultra-modern and rigidly scientific. When one reflects that so many of them have lived abroad as exiles, their ignorance of European conditions and the Western mind is hard to explain. They usually live, however, in their own restricted revolutionary circles. They have little curiosity touching anything outside the Socialist movement. Many of them in London rarely went beyond Whitechapel. An exceptionally able Russian friend of mine, who has lived for twenty years in London, actually reported to Moscow, this August, that we were on the verge of revolution. My own attempts to describe the reality were usually received with a chilly and pitying smile. The blockade has naturally deepened this dangerous darkness.

From this political blunder (no worse, be it said, than the blunders on which the Allies have founded their Russian policy for three years) Moscow went on to a still more fatal military mistake. There was much to be said for rapid action, for London was threatening war if Warsaw were occupied, and the French were pouring in munitions. The obvious thing to do was to make an accomplished fact, and above all to cut the Danzig corridor. The soldiers, and Trotsky with them, were aware of the risk, but they were overruled. The army pushed on, without waiting for its guns, munitions and supplies, and the march on Warsaw was rather a raid than an invasion. Some units covered twenty miles a day for twelve days on end, and in spite of brilliant cavalry work, when the Poles under French leadership repeated the dispositions of the Marne and brought land mines and big guns into play, the invading army was nearly destroyed. Transport, meanwhile, over the broken railways was a grave difficulty, and, for a time, the men on the Polish front were living on half rations.

The sequel showed the realism and originality of the Communist leaders. Anyone else in their place would have brought up reinforcements (which were available) and fought on, at least until they could have ensured a good and equitable frontier on the Curzon line, or something near it. All the conventional reasoning about prestige, to say nothing of territory, argued for such a course. Moscow bluffed with spirit, but I saw enough at headquarters to doubt whether there was ever any real intention of continuing the Polish War. That war had been first of all a necessity, for with the Ukraine in hostile hands the survival of Soviet Russia would have been a nearly insoluble economic problem. The Ukraine, whatever else might happen, had been recovered. For the rest, the sole attraction, the one meaning of the war, had been centred in the hope of a Polish revolution. That did not happen, and when Moscow realized its miscalculation, the war ceased to have any further object. It ignored all considerations of prestige, and offered at Riga half White Russia (excluding Minsk) as the price of peace. Two other considerations had their weight. The harvest had failed, famine would be inevitable unless the railways were free during the winter for civil traffic. In the second place, the threat of Wrangel's advance from the Crimea could no longer be disregarded, and the Russian railway system cannot cope with wars on two fronts at once. He has since been smashed with a swiftness and completeness which show that the Red Army has not lost the efficiency which it displayed in the first half of the Polish campaign.

*   *   *   *   *

The history of this year calls for a commentary. Does it mean that Europe has to face in Russia a neighbour who will never desist from the attempt to promote revolution with bayonets? In that case, of course, the law of self-preservation might justify capitalist Powers in fighting on till the Communist dictatorship were overthrown. Such a conclusion, however, would outrun the facts. If Poland had been a good and pacific neighbour, if Russia had wantonly attacked her in order to force a revolution upon her, then clearly the gravest inference would be warranted. The facts tend all the other way. Poland had pursued towards Russia (as, indeed, towards all her neighbours) a policy of reckless provocation and aggression. So anxious was Moscow to avoid a war that it was willing, before the Polish march on Kiev, to purchase peace with vast territorial concessions. The attempt to force a revolution was a grave blunder, but was essentially a defensive move. There is no reason to suppose that Russia will repeat it, unless she is again provoked by wanton attack.

But what, the reader may say, do you make of Moscow's Eastern policy? Is she not subsidizing the Turkish Nationalists? Has she not sent some kind of Red force into Persia? Did she not, this summer, at Baku, summon a Congress of the Eastern peoples and bid them join her in a revolutionary Holy War? Certainly she has done all these things. Napoleon in a similar situation followed the same tactics. She has as much right, or as little, to invade Persia as Lord Curzon has, and the French only wish that they had been before her in securing the alliance of the Turks. The Baku Congress must have been a most picturesque convention, and that must have been a telling oration of Zinóviev's which caused Moslem chieftains to draw their swords from their scabbards and swear a jehad upon them. None the less, this Eastern policy is not a development of Communism. The basis of Russian propaganda in the East is nationality, and its rallying cry is "Down with Imperialism." Lenin himself made this clear in a note presented to the Third International, and apologized in a rather laboured essay for not preaching social revolution in the East. So true is this, that I even met in Moscow an able Indian Communist who had refused to attend the Baku Congress because its basis was merely the " bourgeois " idea of nationality. This man, an obviously honest extremist, was ill at ease about the whole trend of Russia's Eastern policy, and was deeply disappointed because he could get no support for his own project of preaching a proletarian revolution in India.

The plain fact is, as I gathered in a very free talk with Radek, who had just returned from Baku, that this Eastern policy is purely tactical. It is the obvious offensive-defensive against England. Lenin, like Napoleon, strikes at our most vulnerable spot. Radek, with his dazzling habit of calculated indiscretion, told me many details of the scheme (doubtless with many omissions). The essence of what he said was, however, this, that Moscow disposes absolutely of all levers in this intrigue and controls all the powder trains for this conflagration. She can touch the levers or refrain, exactly as she wills, and stop when she wills, and she will be guided solely by her own interests. To drop metaphor, it is mainly a question of giving subsidies and arms or of ceasing to give them. She will do the one or the other, according as Downing Street chooses peace or war. I have little hesitation in accepting this statement as true. If Russia were preaching Communism in the East, then indeed she might well go on, whatever we might do. Principle, indeed, might require her to go on. But nationality is not her creed. It is a cry which she uses for a temporary tactical end. It would cost her nothing to desist from it.

My own reading of the " armed doctrine " is, then, that it is in actual practice mainly a defensive weapon. Moscow will try to rouse the Western masses, will appeal even to the Eastern tribes, just so long as we blockade her and subsidize the endless series of enemies who attack her. The notion that she prefers war, and consciously bases the dictatorship on continual war, is a gross delusion. On the contrary, three-fourths of her difficulties are due to the continual war. Peace is her only chance of solving her problems of industry, transport and food supply. Every Communist, however fanatical—indeed, every Russian—repeated this thesis to me, till I grew weary of hearing it. But surely, the reader may object, the nation did rally to Moscow during the Polish attack. May not Moscow keep war going in order to exploit this patriotism ? There certainly was a patriotic rally, yet I believe that the nation rallied with much more enthusiasm, much more hope, a much nearer approach to genuine loyalty, during the constructive idyll which preceded the Polish attack.

Russians are not Frenchmen, and the Napoleonic analogy may lead us sadly astray. They do not enjoy war : they never think of glory, and they know only too well that war means famine. I believe firmly that if we could but bring ourselves to give Russia peace, the nation would fling itself into the tasks of education and construction with an ardour and a happiness that would banish the armed doctrine to the dim regions of theory. Years will elapse before her shattered life can be even moderately easy, and many years more before she could realize her high ambition of universal culture and diffused prosperity. She cannot make the world-revolution. The men who can make it, the men whose mad fear of it dooms them to prepare it, are to be sought, not in Moscow, but in Paris. If France continues to prolong the epoch of militarism, if she forbids the Germans to hope, above all, if she ruins their economic life by seizing the Ruhr coalfield, or handing Upper Silesia to Poland, then certainly I foresee another attempt from Moscow to raise revolution in the West. The danger is not a vain imagining, but if it comes it will be of our making. Moscow cannot make a revolution in Europe. She can only reap where we have sowed despair.

CHAPTER IX

THE TWO REVOLUTIONS

IF I could condense into one question the curiosity which urged me to visit Russia, it would be this : How far is the Revolution a constructive and creative movement ? The main fact, however, is an immense and tragic destruction. That the Russian people lives amid great poverty and suffering ; that much is in decay which once seemed to thrive ; that some of the outward aspect of civilization has been worn away—so much I knew in advance, from the lips of Russian friends and from earlier travellers. I should have expected no less, for I had seen something of the economic misery of Poland during the previous year, and most of the causes which brought Warsaw and Lodz so pitiably low had also been at work in Russia. I saw what earlier reports had taught me to expect. The ravages of war were obvious at once in the shell-pitted tracks and the broken bridges on the railway from Esthonia to Petrograd. In the fields the thin crops were being reaped by women and with sickles. The original magnificence of Petrograd only intensified the impression of desolation in its silent, grass-grown streets. One learnt, as one went farther, that the extreme decay of Petrograd was exceptional, but everywhere one encountered in other towns, amid the shabby and underfed inhabitants of neglected streets, evidences of poverty which moved one alternately to pity and to admiration for this stoical and enduring people. It is true that this impression vanished in the country, for the peasants are better fed and in some respects more prosperous than ever before. But it is also true that in the country the Revolution is very far from having accomplished its constructive tasks.

The problem for any clear-headed inquiry is desperately complex. The ruin is a fact. To what causes shall we assign it? How much is due to three years of the Great War and to three years of civil war and foreign intervention? How much is due to the protracted, if incomplete, blockade of the Central Powers, and to that of the Allies? What part of the manifest disorganization must one set down to the carelessness and laziness which are not temporary and communistic, but habitual and Russian? Finally, when these causes are eliminated, how far is the Revolution itself a cause of the breakdown, and, if it be so, must one blame its root principles or ascribe this part of the wreckage only to the first shock of any sudden change?

In this bewilderment I took the course of going forward, trusting to observation and to hints from those with whom I talked, to discover a method of solution. Some of the data are only partly available, for the confusion of the times and the prejudices of observers have obscured and entangled them. The Russian evidence is coloured by propaganda, and when passions run high it should not surprise us to encounter dishonesty as well as prejudice. Neither side is scrupulous, and the " White " exiles are embittered by defeat and their own material losses, and after an absence of three years from Russia they have lost contact with its realities. It has been their misfortune in several cases to accept as authentic, documents which are manifestly forgeries.

One may make a limited use of the comparative method in such an inquiry as this. If one knows that the whole of Central and Eastern Europe has been reduced to a state of poverty and disorganization comparable to that of Russia, one may conclude with some certainty that the causes common to both cases have played a large part in producing the same results. I spent four months during the spring of 1919 in Germany, Austria, Hungary and Poland. When I saw Russia I felt as though some horrible but familiar daylight dream were pursuing me. There was the same dilapidation, the same semi-starvation, the same nakedness, the same sense that a civilization was sinking into a slum existence. One did not need to reason or analyse. One felt the obscene presence of war. There were, of course, many shades and grades in the poverty, as there were within Central Europe itself. Petrograd was depopulated as Vienna is not, but those who remained seemed to me rather less pitiable than the Viennese. Germany, always much richer, more intelligent and more energetic than Russia, had, of course, retained more of its old comfort, but even here the comparison was not all in Germany's favour. The Russian children have suffered less than those of Leipzig or Berlin. All these capitalistic countries had still their small luxurious class, which Russia has wholly lost. But I have no doubt whatever that the working class of the Russian towns is better off than was that of Poland as I saw it. When one recollected that Russia had endured not four but six years of war and blockade, and had received none of the foreign charity and none of the Allied credits which went to Poland and Austria, one could not hesitate to draw the inference. This ruin which stretches from the Rhine to the Urals is the devastation of war.

A few days spent in Esthonia on the way to Petrograd offered a valuable basis for comparison. Geographically, though not racially, Esthonia is a part of Russia. It had felt the full brunt of the Great War and the German blockade, and up to the defeat of Yudénitch had been involved as an ally in the civil war. It had, however, escaped the Revolution, for one may ignore a very brief and very mild period of local Bolshevism, which left no lasting consequences behind it. So far from being blockaded by the Allies, it had enjoyed their favours. In spite of these advantages, its economic plight was pitiable. The Esthonian mark, nominally a shilling, sold on the exchange at the rate of a thousand to the pound sterling. Industry was almost at a standstill; factories worked intermittently, if at all, and one of the biggest textile mills in Europe, at Narva, stood idle. Some timber, flax, paper and potatoes (largely accumulated stocks) were being exported, but the exports were absurdly insufficient, when balanced against the imports of coal, grain, cotton and manufactured goods. Agricultural production had fallen seriously. Formerly the big dairy farms of Esthonia had supplied all the needs of Petrograd. Now their yield was so small that even in Reval butter and milk were scarce and dear. That seemed to be due mainly to the operation of the individualistic agrarian reforms. The big and well-organized estates of the Baltic (German) landlords had been broken up, and the small-holders who had replaced them were proving themselves much less efficient. There was little or no co-operation among them, and the advantages of the former centralized equipment and direction had been lost. It was now no one's business to attend to the drainage of the land or to fight the forest fires, and the land itself was deteriorating. Thanks to the open port, more of the amenities of life were obtainable in Reval than in Moscow, and a fair selection of imported goods, both English and German, could be bought in the market. Even better stocked were the pawnshops and second-hand stores. The prices, however, when translated into Esthonian currency, were beyond the means of the working class, which lived in a state of violent discontent, very near to the margin of starvation, and indulged in periodical general strikes. Even for the middle class, life was uncomfortable and expensive, and one noticed such symptoms as the complete stoppage of the tramways in Reval. Ministries were short-lived, and by all I could learn the new Esthonian official class was grossly corrupt. It lacked the prestige or authority to enforce direct taxation, which was being generally evaded. Business men complained of the lack of confidence, and every one seemed, by hoarding, to be preparing for some imminent catastrophe. Amid the general poverty and disorganization some individuals, however, were thriving, and their coarse revelry rendered the hotels almost uninhabitable. Most of the profits from Esthonia's chief product, flax, went to middlemen and foreign syndicates. At a time when flax sold in the world market for £240, the price which the local farmer obtained for it was only £35 per ton.

This fragment of Russia saved for Capitalism is not yet a shining example of its benefits, and it testifies to the power of war to break down civilization.

*   *   *   *   *

One need not, however, trust to comparisons. There are records which describe the condition of Russia during the year 1917, before the Social Revolution had begun. The ablest of the correspondents who were in Russia in the early months of 1917 was, to my thinking, Michael Farbman, of the *Manchester Guardian*, an observer who unites a tolerant and liberal mind with a trained ability to study economic conditions. A lecture, afterwards republished, which he delivered in London in July 1917 on " The Russian Revolution and the War " is peculiarly valuable, because its date removes it from the category of controversial writings. Written as it was, three months before Lenin seized power, it cannot be dismissed as a retrospective apology for Bolshevik disorganization. While Tsardom still existed, the Army, he tells us, had begun " to disintegrate, to rot away. Soldiers began to desert *en masse* for the rear, returning to their villages . . . . The whole civil structure was in a state of dangerous decay. Favouritism and corruption flourished as never before in Russia." He goes on to describe, with instances, how bankers and industrialists made their legendary profits at the expense of the nation. The officials bullied and terrorized the bankers under threats of arrest and levied blackmail upon these " marauders of the rear." A Commission of Investigation was appointed, which in its turn took hush-money (as subsequent trials proved) from the bankers. " The whole economy of State was conducted on

11

lines of plunder. . . . To borrow money and exploit the printing-press—this was the sum total
of the financial wisdom of Tsardom," and while
"the mad dance of paper millions went on," the
wives and children of the soldiers "actually died
of hunger." The peasants were, indeed, saving
money, but owing to the rising prices could no
longer buy

the necessaries of the peasant life and work—vehicles, horse-
shoes, nails, ropes, shoes, clothing. In consequence, the
longer the war went on, the more reluctant they became to
sell their grain. Money had become useless to them ; they
would have been glad to exchange their grain for the things
they needed, but these they could not buy in the market,
and the State was unable to provide them. The result was
that the peasants began to hoard, and even to hide their
stocks of grain for a rainy day, all the more so as the crops
were diminishing every year of the war.

This reduction of the crops was due to the mobilization
of the men, the requisition of the horses and the
diminution, through wear and tear, of agricultural
machinery, which could not be replaced. "Soon
actual dearth ensued. It was steadily augmented by
three factors : actual diminution of yield, the depre-
ciation of the currency and the breakdown of transport." On that last head Mr. Farbman adds some
details. War inevitably made a shortage of rolling
stock, but "the utter collapse of the railway system"
was due to "the crazy mismanagement of the
authorities." When, in 1915, reinforcements were
urgently needed for Warsaw, both lines were used
for traffic in the same direction. There ensued a
stupendous block of empty trains, and the congestion
was relieved by hurling everything over the embank-
ments and scrapping enormous quantities of rolling

stock.   Thanks to the dilapidation, waste and capture of railway material, " the carrying capacity of the railways fell so low . . . that the Government would prohibit all passenger traffic in certain zones for a week or a fortnight." None the less, " the food shortage assumed dangerous dimensions," and as early as 1916 the Government had begun to requisition grain forcibly in the villages.

This graphic picture of the condition of Russia in the early weeks of 1917 is almost in itself a sufficient answer to those who suppose that Communism caused the present breakdown.   It was, on the contrary, the breakdown which led to revolution. There was no improvement under Kérensky.   Writing of the position in May 1917, Mr. Farbman says : " The financial position had become still more acute. The economic situation, food supply and transport had almost reached the point of catastrophe." Kérensky was an orator, who tried to substitute phrases for organization, and under him sheer anarchy set in.   The Tsarist police was disbanded, and robbery and murder became so common that passers-by would barely pause to notice a corpse in the street.   In the earlier stages of the Communist Revolution this anarchy continued.   Everyone had arms, and the bandits, who often posed as anarchists, even possessed motor-cars, machine guns and field pieces.   It was not until the Extraordinary Commission was created to cope with it, in the spring of 1918, that outward order was restored.   Meanwhile, the war and the blockade assumed other forms.   Throughout the period of the Great War the Turks had closed the Black Sea.   The Germans also closed the Baltic to traffic from the West.   The enemy blockade, it is true, was not absolute, for

Vladivostok and the Arctic ports were open, but as the railways became hopelessly congested, the supplies which reached these distant ports remained to cumber the sheds and the sidings. It is broadly true that from 1914 to 1920 Russia has been cut off from the supplies of the English, German and American machinery and tools on which she had always depended, from American cotton and English coal, as well as from the manufactures of Poland, and latterly of her former sea-board provinces. Timber could not be cut for lack of saws; paper could not be made because the "nets" used in treating the wood pulp were worn out; spare parts were lacking for the locomotives, and even before the Revolution there was a paralysing shortage of such simple things as nuts and bolts, nails and screws.

It was a country already ruined and worn out that the Allies now proceeded to "save" by military intervention and subsidized civil war. Of the working of these causes of disintegration I have given many illustrations, but it may be worth while to draw attention to one or two general aspects.

Firstly, one must recollect that throughout these three years the Bolsheviks were waging continual war without the possibility of resorting either to foreign or domestic loans. No civilized belligerent in modern times has ever been in this position. Tsarist Russia had run into debt to the other Allies for a great part of her munitions and equipment, and the "White" armies were entirely dependent on foreign supplies. Apart from what they captured, the Reds had to rely solely on their own industry. This means that the evident failure to produce clothing and implements for civilian needs did not imply an absolute collapse of industry. Some factories and foundries were working, busily and well, but they were working mainly for the Army. I was told more than once by high authorities that in 1920 the production of munitions was as high as it had been in 1916, when the Tsarist maximum was reached. Again, the relative failure of the Soviet Government to maintain an adequate food supply has a simple geographical explanation, apart from other economic causes. Up to the end of 1919, that is to say for two years, it was in secure possession only of Central and Northern Russia, a region which never in modern times had been self-supporting. Tsardom, if it had been cut óff from the Ukraine, the Don and Volga basins, the Caucasus and Siberia, would probably have come much nearer to general starvation than Communism ever did. In these outer regions, moreover, lay most of the fuel (all the oil and nearly all the coal), most of the metals and all the cotton on which industry depended. Even after the reconquest of these distant provinces their resources were not at once available, partly because the rolling stock of the railways was worn out by the strain of six years of war, partly because the bridges and traffic yards had been wrecked by the ". Whites," and partly because they had deliberately destroyed much of the machinery of the mines. Towns which lay in the zone of the civil war were stripped of their industrial machinery as each side retreated, and much of it was lost. It is impossible in such a problem as this to apply exact quantitative tests, but to my thinking the ruin due to the two wars and the two blockades is alone sufficient to account for most of the present dilapidation in Russia.

*   *   *   *   *

Beyond a doubt, the first impact of the Revolution upon the social and industrial structure of this country already in collapse did but aggravate the ruin. The armies demobilized themselves, and the millions of armed men, flinging themselves upon the broken railway system, carried their own demoralization with them and destroyed in the process much of the remaining rolling stock. In many factories the workmen broke up the machinery and sold it, sometimes intact, sometimes as scrap metal. The same thing happened in the country, and valuable breeding studs of horses and pedigree cattle were carried off by the peasants from the more modern farms. There seems to be in the character of the primitive races of Eastern Europe a positive zest in destruction. We have borrowed from them the word " pogrom," which means, literally, a smashing. I saw, in 1913, the meteorological observatory near Sofia as the Rumanian Army had left it. Every instrument had been elaborately smashed, evidently with a sort of luxurious pleasure, and I remember wondering whether English or French or German soldiers would have enjoyed breaking up beautiful and costly apparatus. The Bolsheviks took great pains to protect artistic treasures, I believe with fair success, but they had as yet no organization capable of controlling the conduct of remote villages. One cannot blame the party directly for these happenings, though it may be said that it had an indirect responsibility, since it had evoked the passion of hate and broken down the restraint of habit. More serious by far than these excesses were the unfortunate results of committee rule in the workshops. The Russian workmen were not ripe for collective responsibility in production, and some of the decline in output and the slackening of organization must be ascribed to rash experiments in industrial democracy. So much the Communists have themselves recognized, and one-man management is now the rule in the daily conduct of all factories, though the general direction of policy is still in the hands of the workers, partly through the shop councils and partly through the trade unions. Most of the exiles and the foreigners who quitted Russia saw the Revolution only during this destructive and unorganized phase, and to them is due the still prevalent belief that Russia is in a state of anarchy.

An anarchical element there was, and in some outlying parts of Russia it is still active. It was not the leaders, nor even the rank and file of the Communist party who inspired it. Their watchword is always " Discipline," and it would be much more reasonable to criticize them for the sharpness of their discipline than for any licence to anarchy. The Communists are essentially Western in their outlook, and they stand for order, authority and creative work. The anarchical element is Russian, Eastern, and entirely spontaneous, a tendency always latent in the unschooled Russian soul. The revolts which are recorded in Russian history, before the advent of Socialism, were always of this " smashing," unconstructive type. Such were the Cossack risings under Stenka Rasin in the seventeenth and under Pugatchév in the eighteenth century. The latter aimed at creating a " peasant Empire," and wherever he marched he liberated the serfs in field, factory and mine, slaughtered the landlords and divided their estates. That was in 1773, but the memory of his immense massacres and burnings remains, and the peasants of the Volga preserve the legend of

his two years' rebellion. The various semi-brigand
leaders who sprang up recently in Southern Russia,
and especially in the Ukraine, continued this primitive,
native, Russian tradition of revolt. There is Petliura,
once a Social Revolutionary and the General of
Ukrainian nationalism, who eventually went over to
the Poles. His speciality is anti-Jewish pogroms.
There was Grigóriev, also originally a Social Revolutionary, who sometimes served and sometimes
revolted against the Moscow Government. He, too,
massacred Jews, and his cruelties at Odessa are
notorious. He was murdered at last by his lieutenant,
Makhnó, who is said to be an anarchist, in so far as he
has any theoretical creed. He also slaughters Jews,
plays the part of a Robin Hood and is said to be
immensely popular with the peasants. He sometimes fought the Red armies, and even massacred
Communists, but he also opposed Deníkin and
Wrangel. He objects to any regular or civilized
government, " smashes " for choice, fights and loots as
a guerrilla, and reflects the untaught, native, peasant
view of freedom and the people's cause. These
heroes flourish in the South, partly because Communism is weak there and partly because in the
South there is still much to loot. The same kind
of unconstructive, wrecking uprising had made
its appearance on a smaller scale during the abortive
Revolution in 1905-6, but it was not formidable,
because arms were not then plentiful in Russia, as
they are now. In wide regions of Southern Russia the
peasants stormed the proprietor's house, pillaged it
and frequently burned it, drove him away, and
proceeded to divide the land among themselves.
Thereafter village society split visibly into its three
groups, the paupers, the " middle " peasants and the

rich peasants, and the last were sometimes despoiled as the landlord had been. The Bolsheviks, who at this period worked only among the industrial proletariat, had nothing whatever to do with these events.

This *jacquerie* recommenced under Kérensky. During the previous generation the position of the peasantry had not improved. The rich peasants were certainly growing richer, and Stolypin's agrarian law of 1909, which aimed at destroying the traditional system of communal land ownership (the *mir*), had begun to evolve a class of moderately prosperous small farmers. But the peasants, as a whole, were growing poorer. The arrears of the land tax showed an alarming tendency to increase, while the number of horses, cattle and sheep per hundred inhabitants was falling sharply (in the last instance from 78 to 40). In the generation which followed the emancipation, the amount of food produced in its ratio to the population had fallen by 7 per cent.[1] The war may have put paper money into the pockets of the peasants, but it diminished still further, and on a gigantic scale, the amount of livestock and the yield of the land. The landlords were heavily indebted ; few had the capital, the enterprise or the knowledge to cultivate scientifically, and they seem to have relied largely upon mean devices, by which they exploited the penury, the ignorance and the thriftlessness of the poorer peasantry. The supposed agricultural riches of Russia were largely mythical, and even on the famous black-earth zone of the South the average yield of the land per acre was about half what the German farmer gets by good

[1] See Sir Donald Mackenzie Wallace's *Russia* (1912) and also Professor Mavor's able *Economic History of Russia*.

husbandry from his sandy soil. The peasants survived by flocking into the artificial industries which sprang up behind Count Witte's wall of high Protection.

The first effect of the Revolution, when it gave the land to the peasants, was to send these half-industrialized countrymen back to their villages. They were not townsmen by choice or ancestry or long habit. They preferred village life. Very often they had retained their rights, as members of the rural commune, to some strips of the common soil. They had left it only because they could not get a living from it. The Revolution promised them an enlarged holding on which they would be able to live, and they began to quit their slums and their barrack dwellings to claim their share of the soil. This return to the land had set in even before the Bolshevik Revolution, for " the land for the peasants " was the declared policy even of Kérensky's Governments. Everyone wanted to be on the spot when the expected division should take place, and many of the soldiers deserted from the Army because they feared that their absence from the village would prejudice their claims. The effect upon industry was naturally disastrous, and the shortage of labour is to-day often as serious a cause of its breakdown as the lack of fuel and raw materials. The Communists proclaimed the dictatorship of the proletariat, but in its hour of triumph the proletariat itself began to vanish under their eyes. They had made a Marxist revolution, but the more fundamental fact was that a spontaneous agrarian revolution was taking place around them and below them, a movement inspired by none of their ideals, a primitive, formless, leaderless impulse of land hunger.

That a Marxist Social revolution should have broken out in Russia at all was an anomaly. It should have happened, on the Marxist reading of history, in a country where capitalist industry had reached its maximum development. Even without a blockade and a civil war, the agrarian revolution would have had a disturbing effect on the whole economy of town life. The normal relation of town to country is not one of simple exchange—manufactured goods against the produce of the fields. The country, in effect, pays a tribute to the towns. Its taxes are largely expended there by the Government ; its rents in great part are carried there by the landlord class ; and one must reckon also the interest on mortgages and the profits of the middlemen who handle the crops. Under all these heads the countryman, in fact, sends to the towns a quantity of grain for which he receives no return in manufactured goods. This entire tribute ceased with the Revolution—the taxes, the rent, the interests and the profits. The peasant had freed himself from obligations to which he had been broken in by centuries of habit. If the towns were to receive the same amount of food as before, they would have to pay for it by manufacturing, not less, but more than of old. Exactly the same thing happened in the French Revolution, and the hunger from which Paris suffered was largely the result of the stoppage of the tribute which the feudal landed class had drawn from the soil. In Russia, as in France, the agrarian revolution in practice followed individualistic lines. The communistic agriculture which the Bolsheviks wished to organize could not be created by the mere fact of desiring it or preaching it. The peasant wanted to own and cultivate his own bit of ground in his own traditional way, and on the whole he has had his will. The plain fact is that the Russian Revolution is communistic only in the towns, and the towns seem doomed by the operation of this blind agrarian upheaval, which no power of human will could possibly have controlled. If the urban civilization of Russia is in danger, one should blame, not the Communism of the Revolution, but rather its inevitable compromise with the opposite principle. It will save itself only if it is able, as the years go on, to industrialize agriculture.

*   *   *   *   *

Another tremendous disadvantage remains to be enumerated among the handicaps which the Bolsheviks accepted when they made a Communist revolution in Russia. They have skipped the intermediate stage of Liberal capitalistic development, and the result is that the human material with which they are working, has a character formed by serfdom and by a low-grade agriculture which still retained the habits of serfdom.

Nearly every foreigner who has seen much of the Russians finds them a lovable and charming people. Their cleverness and genius in many directions, especially in all æsthetic matters, is also recognized by those who know them best. But no words can depict adequately their laziness, carelessness, unpunctuality and inaccuracy, their want of enterprise, their wasteful habits and their inability to organize. That is true, more or less, of all Slavs, and the exceptions are the Czechs, who have lived for centuries under German rule, and the Bulgarians, who are only partly Slav. Even in Poland, which is Catholic and Western, most of such organization as there is is due to baptized Jews or to natives of Posen who have had a German training. Russia, in the old days, was held together largely by the German Balts in the Army and civil service, or else by German and English immigrants or by Jews. These foreign elements are all removed to-day, and the only available substitutes are either the native Jews or Russians who have lived abroad and lost their inbred apathy.

I used to be amazed by the neglected condition of the few gardens which one finds in Russia. When I spoke of this, the answer was, " We should stifle if we lived in the tidiness of Holland or England." One noticed continually things which were sinking into dilapidation—a railway carriage, for example, or a bath-room—when a few minutes' work with a screwdriver would have sufficed to repair them. I used to watch the drivers on the primitive country roads with a mixture of annoyance and admiration. One saw some big obstacle in the way, usually a large stone, which some might call a small rock. Almost any English driver would have got down and rolled it away. The Russian contrived somehow to circumnavigate it. Rather than remove it he would drive through the ditch or over a ploughed field. With a jolt, at an angle which defied gravitation, with groaning springs and straining horses, we somehow got past it. I arrived, after many experiences, at the conviction that the boulder always had been there. Generations of Russian drivers had gone round it. It had defied Ivan the Terrible and Peter the Great, and the odds are that it will survive Lenin. Again, it is often difficult in Russia to obtain sufficient farmyard manure. It struck me that where everyone burns wood, wood

ashes ought to be abundant. No one seemed aware
of their value as a fertilizer or ever dreamed of using
them. At last, I discovered that the principle was
in reality well understood. In the forest regions
of the North the peasants make periodical clearings,
cut down and remove the better trees, burn all the
rest in a vast bonfire and then lightly plough in the
ashes. The result is often wonderful crops for
several years. But to collect wood ashes and apply
them regularly to the land would be too much trouble.
This wastefulness is typical. Russians are fond of
saying that they have " broad minds." They live
in a vast country. They are aware that their own
race is counted by the hundred million. The result
is that this sense of abundance leads them to waste
land, to waste men in war and in peace, and, indeed,
to waste everything in a way which shocks natives
of much richer countries. They tend to do everything on a vast scale, and there is no attention to
detail or economy. With the traditional laziness,
unpunctuality and dirtiness of Russia the Bolsheviks
fight a continual battle. They are probably by far
the most efficient group in Russia. Even in the
worst organized Departments they work distressingly
hard, turn night into day and seem to live without
leisure, rest or recreation. But they work without
system, for they also are Russians. Krassin and
Trotsky, to name only two of the good administrators, are men who have gone through a Western
training.

The explanation of the general Russian inefficiency
is doubtless to be sought in serfdom. The serf was
always comparatively secure, but he had no incentive
to work either well or hard, for even when he was
allowed to go to a town and work as an independent

craftsman, he had to surrender his gains to his owner. Slave labour is always inefficient and wasteful. It is centuries of this system which have formed the character both of the master class and of the peasantry, and of the two the master class was certainly the more incorrigibly worthless. Enterprise, where it did exist, seems usually to have taken shape in forms of dishonesty much cruder than those of the West. Into the life of the average man the economic motives which in the West serve to evoke competence and industry seem hardly to have entered. One puzzle interested me a good deal. Why do Russians, in everything else so inexact, shine in music, the exactest of all the arts ? Why is a Russian opera not merely a masterpiece of taste and expression, but also competent, punctual and orderly, as little else in Russia is ? I suppose the answer is that a man, if he has normal vitality and good physical parts, can do well what he really wants to do. Music interests this race : business and the routine of life do not. It has never lived under conditions which obliged it, or stimulated it, to apply its brains to production or administration. It seems to be fully alive only when it turns to the arts. It may be fortunate for Communism that the Western commercial mentality which measures every value in money gain was always weak among the mass of Russians. But it is a terrible handicap that it had to launch its tremendous experiments among a slothful and inefficient nation. Half the battle of the Bolsheviks is a battle with national habits.

*   *   *   *   *

I do not know how to carry this analysis further.

The man who ignores the part which the Great War, the civil war and the blockade have played in producing the present collapse of Russian industry has not begun to face realities. The man who attributes to these causes the whole of the collapse comes much nearer to the truth. But I add, as a fourth and a fifth to these fatal three, the sudden shock of the social revolution and the slower effects of the agrarian revolution.

The Bolsheviks destroyed the very little that was still left in 1917 of the old fabric of order, and six months elapsed before they succeeded in reconstructing a policed society. In the villages the anarchic interval was often longer, for in many districts the swift uprising of the whole peasantry against the landed class was followed by a more protracted struggle of the poorer against the richer peasants. The loss of all the skilled foreign direction of labour was serious, but this had begun in 1914, when the Germans were displaced, to the great injury of every department of Russian life which they had penetrated. There followed the emigration of a portion of the Russian upper and middle class, to the number, it is said, of some two million persons, men, women and children. The importance of this loss may be exaggerated, for many of these " White " exiles are drones and parasites, who never produced anything—receivers of rent, speculative financiers, middlemen and military adventurers—but there is a minority among them of men who were useful as organizers and technical experts. They fled in most cases from choice and not from necessity. It is a mistake to suppose that the upper bourgeoisie was ever proscribed as a class, even at the height of the Terror. There are many important and conspicuous

members of it who are still in Moscow, ex-Ministers
of the Tsarist regime, prominent " Cadet " deputies,
bankers and members of powerful industrial families,
and these men, though discontented and critical,
continue to live safely and in relative comfort,
and they may even be found filling some fairly
important posts under the Soviet Government.
Some of this loss by emigration might have been
avoided if both sides, during these early months,
had had a clearer vision of the future. The
Revolution released a pent-up flood of hatred
in the working class towards the exceptionally
worthless ruling and possessing class of Russia. It
is a perversion, however, to regard the Communists
as the authors of this hate. It had been in the
making for centuries, and the makers of it were the
old landed class which had traded in serfs, the new
industrial class which had grown rich on cheap
labour, and the corrupt and oppressive bureaucracy.

It is easy in retrospect to censure or regret this
hatred. Nothing is gained in a social revolution,
and very much may be lost, by an effort to degrade
the former possessing class and to lower its standards
below a civilized level of comfort. The central aim
is to gain control and possession, for the whole
community, of the means of production. The less
there is of " smashing," conflict, disturbance and
offence in the process, the better will the prospect
for the future be. Mere equality in wealth is not
a constructive or satisfying social ideal, and much
inequality might be tolerated in the transition stage,
if civil war can thereby be avoided. It would have
been wise from the first to make the new conditions
tolerable, even to the less worthy members of the
class which suffered by the Revolution. But all the

12

elements in this tragedy of the dispossessed lay already in Russia's past. The upper class and part of the middle class had made themselves hated. As for the Communists, if they had had that balancing and accommodating temper which compromises readily and conciliates opponents, they would never have made a revolution at all.

I think, then, that the shock of revolution must be included among the causes of Russia's decline. Even more important was the disorganization of industry and the decline in agricultural efficiency due to the agrarian revolution—a movement entirely distinct from Communism, and so all-powerful in the country that the Communists could only bend to it and strive to deflect it gradually into courses which might lead to their goal. In practice and effect the agrarian changes were individualistic, and a decline in production followed in Russia, precisely as it has done in Esthonia and in Rumania, and for the same reasons. The system of small-holdings will always mean retrogression in agriculture,[1] unless it is balanced by an elaborate organization of co-operation. The yield from the soil had diminished during the war; it fell still further after and probably because of the agrarian revolution, while much land

---

[1] The reader familiar with Prince Kropotkin's writings may demur. Kropotkin surely took a fallacious example when he argued from the prosperity of the Paris market-gardeners. They grow rich by producing dainties out of season for the luxury market. No one who has ever lived or worked in the country would suggest that it would be an economical plan to raise grain, or " main crop " potatoes, or turnips for fodder, by the methods of small hand cultivation. Moreover, even when he thrives, the small-holder has to work inhumanly hard. In any event, Russian peasants do not apply French methods.

went out of cultivation in the Polish borderland, the Ukraine and other regions cursed by the civil war.[1] The final result is a decline of about 45 per cent. in the production of food from the soil, and it is plainly a combination of war, civil war and agrarian individualism which explains it. This phenomenon is not peculiar to Russia, and the decrease in the productivity of the soil in Germany during the war was much more serious.

Of these five main causes of disturbance and decline in Russia, one only, the sudden shock and anarchy of the early months, is due to the social revolution. This early destructive phase ended, however, in 1918. Since then the will of the Revolution has been bent upon construction, and enough has been attempted, in spite of the handicap of the unending civil war, to rank it among the creative movements of history.

[1] Mr. Michael Farbman has given the Russian figures (*Manchester Guardian*, December 20, 1920). Up to the year 1917 there was a decrease of 10 per cent. in the area cultivated. Since 1917 there has been a further decrease in area of 23 per cent. The average yield per acre has decreased 12 per cent. since 1913. The decrease in the productivity of the soil in Germany between 1914 and 1919 was 40 per cent. (See Professor Starling's Report on Food Conditions in Germany, Cmd. 280.)

CHAPTER X

THE CREATIVE WILL

WHEN I returned from Russia, I noticed that the questions of my friends were framed on two distinct models. Some would open our first conversation with the query, " Well, must we go and do likewise ? " Others would inquire, " Will the Bolsheviks survive ? " The two types of question reveal very distinct lines of approach to the Russian problem, and the time has come to sum up my answers. The former question was rarely present to my own thoughts. On my reading of history, volition and choice play a comparatively small part in the making of revolutions. If ever a day should come when the British Empire lies in ruins ; if our fleets have been shattered without the glory even of a great defence ; if our rulers and statesmen have been overwhelmed by scandal and shame ; if working men and women must take their stand in the bread queues at midnight to secure the bare chance of receiving a loaf for the next day's breakfast, then, indeed, the question whether we shall make a revolution will be urgent and actual. But in that day it will matter little how we answer it. The agitator who desires revolution will be a passive thing borne along by the flood, and the philosopher who would withstand it, a bubble on its froth. Until a State begins to near these conditions of moral and economic collapse, to discuss the gains and losses of revolution is an academic exercise, and to preach it is to waste one's labour, if it be nothing worse. The Russians themselves hardly realize how peculiar were the conditions in which their revolution succeeded. The industrial population helped them because it was starving. The peasants helped them because they wanted land. The Army helped them because it was defeated and war-weary. Even in Central Europe, where there is the same semi-starvation and the same psychology of defeat, I incline to think the success of a social revolution unlikely, firstly, because a mercenary army has been substituted for the nation in arms, and secondly, because the peasantry is law-abiding. Even when, as in Italy, both moral and economic conditions favour revolution, it is barely thinkable, for the obvious reason that Italy would go under in two or three months for lack of coal and corn. One might go on accumulating circumstances which destroy any possible parallel. What comparison can there be between the mentality of the unlettered Russian peasant, himself the son or grandson of a serf, his mind a cultural blank into which any propaganda may be poured, and the English workman whose family traditions and habits of thought have been fixed in Church and State by three centuries of Liberal teaching ? The man who would base his tactics in America, England or France on Russian experience must be innocent alike of history, economics and geography. If a break ever comes in our smooth constitutional development, then, it seems to me, we should do well to think out our own problems entirely afresh. The Russian parallel is so peculiar that any attempt to model ourselves upon it could only mislead.

*   *   *   *   *

The Communist Revolution in Russia was, to my thinking, the desperate effort of a society in the last stages of dissolution and despair to reconstruct itself upon a new foundation. Never was there in history a revolution so manifestly inevitable.

"Everything in history," it may be objected, "is inevitable, but let us, for argument's sake, vary the accidental factors. If the Allies had not driven Russia into the disastrous offensive of July, if Kérensky had been a stronger or Lenin a less forceful man, were social revolution and civil war really inevitable ? " I think they were, and I believe that they were latent in the agrarian position, apart altogether from the folly of the Allies, the weakness of Kérensky and the determination of Lenin. The peasant masses had been bent since 1905 on owning the land and enlarging their miserable holdings. All the parties of the Left were pledged to the immediate nationalization of the land, and all of them refused even to consider the question of compensation for the owners. I often wonder whether Allied statesmen, soldiers and editors who conspire in Paris and London with Social Revolutionaries, and talk of Mensheviks as respectable moderates, realize that neither of these parties had in their programmes, their speeches, their Press or their drafts of legislation a whit more respect for the sanctity of private property, at all events in land, than the Bolsheviks themselves. Indeed, the agrarian law which they enforced had actually been drafted by the Social

Revolutionary Centre leader, Victor Tchernóv, and was rapidly passed by the Constituent Assembly during its few hours of life. Now, in Russia the only property which matters much is land, and to dispossess the landed class uncompensated was in itself to make a revolution. If Lenin had behaved with the utmost constitutional propriety, Russia would none the less have been, by the early months of 1918, in the full tide of agrarian revolution.

Violence also was inevitable. The Koltcháks and the Wrangels, be it remembered, were very much alive at this date. The first of them, Kornílov, had preceded Lenin in his attempt at a *coup d'état*. Conceive the incidents that must have followed the sudden application of this sweeping law in an anarchic country. There would have been in any event a *jacquerie*, and a flight of a desperate, penniless landed class to the towns. Would Koltchák, who dissolved the remains of the Constituent Assembly in Siberia and shot several of its members, have hesitated to do as much in Russia ? The dispossessed aristocracy would have fought Kérensky as gladly as it fought Lenin. It did not fight for democracy. It fought for land.

" But still," it may be said, " at least Mensheviks and Social Revolutionaries would not have laid their hands on Russian industry as the Bolsheviks did, and the present economic ruin would have been avoided," Even that is doubtful, for in the cities the workmen had created their factory committees and were struggling for control long before the October Revolution. The Mensheviks accept in principle the doctrine of the proletarian dictatorship. I fail to see how any professedly Socialist party could nationalize land and still treat private property in factories as sacred. On that issue the Social Revolutionaries, the biggest party in the Assembly, would probably have split, as they have since done, into three irreconcilable factions, the Left virtually Communist and the Right practically Liberal. But, once more, the decay of industry was a fatal consequence of the agrarian policy. The most obvious and grievous cause of the breakdown in Russia to-day is the shortage of labour, even more than the lack of fuel or raw materials. Mobilization and the food shortage are partly to blame, but the chief cause of it is that the industrial workmen have gone home to enjoy their land in their villages. Russian industry had existed on the basis of the penury of village life. It was the exactions of landlord and tax-gatherer and the scarcity of land which drove the surplus peasant population into the towns. The factory was bound to feel the effects of the revolution in the village. If no one had talked " dictatorship," if no one had expropriated the factory owners, the main economic phenomena of to-day would still have been apparent. Russia, if it had escaped the blockade, would have become a colony exporting food and raw materials and importing from the West the things which its industry could no longer produce. Russian industry was always an artificial creation, fenced by high tariffs, located in the most absurd places, far from the sources of fuel and materials, and surviving only because the landless peasantry gave it an inexhaustible supply of cheap labour. The agrarian revolution struck at its roots.

This strange chapter of the Russian Revolution, as it unfolds itself to me, is then the story of an inevitable agrarian upheaval, with a no less inevitable civil war and the decline of industry as its sequels.

My firm belief is that under Communist rule the anarchy and suffering of this transition period have been combated, in some respects with relative success, by the Communists, where every other party would have failed. True, they challenged the hostility of the Allies and the whole capitalist world more recklessly than any other party would have done. On the other hand, after meeting some of the leaders of the other parties, I find myself wholly unable to imagine their survival, even for a few months, under half the dangers and the miseries which the Communists have surmounted during three years. The Menshèvik leaders, whose party was never large and never touched the peasants, are men of obvious sincerity and a noble if somewhat passive courage, able theorists and shrewd if negative critics, but they seemed to me to lack entirely the dæmonic will, the driving force, the tactical instinct and the constructive power of their rivals. The Social Revolutionaries were, in their early and more admirable phase, sentimentalists and idealists with a dreamy Socialistic nationalism and a queer Slav trick of idealizing the peasant : as they gained power and popularity they were swamped by an opportunist element and their big party lost its unity. It was not merely the strong and reckless will and the firm discipline of the Communists which gave them their advantage. They had the better strategic position. They had the majority (as the Constituent Assembly election proved) in the two capitals, in the Northern armies and in North and Central Russia generally. The concentrated industrial population followed them. They controlled, in short, the centres of power and the vital routes of communication, and when it came to civil war, they could

fight on "internal lines." The Social Revolutionaries, apart from their disunion and their poor
leadership, had to rely on a peasant following,
scattered in the villages, which they could not
mobilize, and their main strength lay in the outlying
provinces of the Empire, remote from each other
and the centre. The Communists, then, were alone
able to hold the centre, and from this base they
have gradually recovered the fringes of Russia. Their
main advantage, however, in grappling with the
economic problem lay in the fact that they are,
in spite of the good education and even gentle birth
of a few of their leaders, a genuine proletarian party,
as the others are not. They are doing things to-day
which no Tsar, and certainly no Kérensky, dare even
have conceived. They have introduced the principle
of labour conscription in order to drag the skilled
workmen out of the villages and to keep them in
the factories.

Russians are so much accustomed to the idea of
conscription that they do not resent a summons to
leave the village and work in a factory as violently
as British workmen would. They know that the
community has dire need of their skilled labour, and
they realize that no private interest profits by this
interference with their personal liberty. What they
do bitterly resent, however, is that in the factory
they are not fed so amply as in the village—indeed,
they may sometimes be half-starved. That is the
reason for the continual strikes, usually of a day's
duration. Overtime is not nearly so serious a matter
as it is commonly represented to be. The normal
working day for manual labour is fixed in Russia at
eight hours. In the Soviet offices clerical workers do
only six hours, which also is the limit for all

juvenile workers, and for mothers who are nursing their own infants. It is a fact, however, that during the Polish War men in factories working for the Army were sometimes expected to give two or even four hours of overtime daily—of course for very high pay. This was an emergency measure; but even so, I found in the Vladímir factories, most of which were working for the Army, that the overtime was limited by rule to fifty hours per month. That does not seem excessive in the circumstances. It is grossly untrue to suggest that a twelve-hour day is usual or even common, but undoubtedly the labour discipline is severe. It is imposed, however, by the trade unions and not by an employer, or even directly by the State. " Personal liberty," as a witty Russian said to me, " is an article of primary necessity. It must therefore be rationed." There is little enough of it for general consumption. The Communists deal drastically with strikes, evoke the energies of the workers by extra food rations, pay by piece rates and make the life of a lazy workman a burden to him. It is an unamiable task. It can be defended, as was the rather similar tampering with liberty in our own Munitions Act, only as a means of social self-preservation in the direst of extremities. It is the action of a ship's captain on a wreck, who draws his revolver to control the crew. It is possible for the Bolsheviks to do it only because their title to be the party of the workers is unquestionable. It could not be done if any vestige of private profit survived in industry. It can be done only because the Bolsheviks have visibly abolished all the privileges of the rich and won the gratitude of the workers by their positive constructive policy. These emergency remedies are not

Communism.   They are harsh expedients designed
to cope with a hideous crisis, which only a party of
working men could possibly have imposed upon the
mass of working men.

*   *   *   *   *

The Bolsheviks have, in their tremendous adventure, entirely discarded democracy as the West
understands it.   I question whether any party
could have ridden the storm of the agrarian revolution and the civil war, with the ruin caused by
the World War as its scene, without departing widely
from the principles and practice of democracy.   I
think it unlikely that the Constituent Assembly,
with its many violently hostile groups, could have
been welded into a workable governing chamber.
A coalition would have been powerless for energetic
action.   But let us ask ourselves frankly what we
mean by democracy in such a country as Russia.
One may mean, of course, that certain groups of
intellectuals, clever, well-educated and gifted with
the power of speech, should somehow use the
machinery of elections in order to guide the State
in accordance with their own more or less enlightened ideas.   That is not democracy, though it may
respect democratic forms.   In quiet and normal
times, amid relative prosperity, if no violent Left
or Right wing groups had undermined the moderates,
they might perhaps have managed to rule on their
own lines with a show of Liberalism.   But the
convinced democrat must surely mean more than this.
Allow what you will for the leadership of the better-
educated groups and the inspiration of exceptional
men, the main lines of your policy must have some
affinity with the mind of the numerous mass.   In

England, the three organized parties may think a little more actively and a little more rigidly than the average elector, but there is no wide gap and no sheer contradiction between them and him. His ideas, rather more sharply formulated, are their ideas. Nothing of this kind is possible in Russia, with its illiterate peasant mass living in the dense ignorance and the crass superstition of the Middle Ages. If democracy means giving the majority the sort of government which it wants, that government would have been neither Menshevik nor Bolshevik, neither Social Revolutionary nor " Cadet " nor yet Tsarist. A genuine peasant programme would certainly have included peace, and that at any price. It would then have demanded not land nationalization, but the division of the land and peasant ownership, without one rouble of compensation to the landlords. Its next plank would have been free trade in food, or, in other words, the unlimited exploitation of the towns by the peasant profiteer. It would have resisted passively every sort of centralization and every effort of the enlightened minority by pressure or encouragement to raise the standard of cultivation. I doubt if it wanted much to be done for education, and I am sure it wanted no hygienic advance. It would have persecuted the Jews, cold-shouldered the intellectuals and cringed to the ghostly terrorism of the priests, while objecting strongly to their exactions. It would have meant the slow death of the towns and the extinction of civilization. In the end it would have prepared Russia for colonial exploitation either by the Germans or the West. That, if the peasants had had the will or the skill to express their minds, would have been the " democratic " policy.

This chapter in Russian history is puzzling, I think, both for the friends and the enemies of the Bolsheviks, because few realize the true character of their achievement. They are trying by a heroic exercise of will to turn this spontaneous Russian agrarian revolution into a Western Communist revolution. Gradually the agitator evolved into the constructive statesman ; the negative, wrecking peasant tendency was repressed and the more positive creative instincts of the civilized urban artisan gained the upper hand. They could triumph only by a firm dictatorship, and it is essentially a dictatorship of the urban proletariat over the backward country-side.

In one sense the Bolsheviks are not in much danger. Soviet rule runs, I should say, less risk of overthrow in the early future than Parliamentary democracy in Germany or Constitutional monarchy in Italy. On the other hand, the dictatorship is still a precarious adventure, because it is doubtful how far it can achieve its own constructive aims. The broad fact is, to-day, that the peasantry alone lives in comparative comfort and is well fed. Industry is dwindling and the industrial proletariat lives on half-rations. Save for the few Soviet farms and the still fewer communal farms, the land has not in any real sense been socialized. Whatever the law may say, the fact in all essentials is peasant ownership, qualified by a State monopoly of grain, which succeeds in irritating the peasants without adequately feeding the towns. The educational efforts of the Communists have made an immense and rapid advance, alike in the schools for children, the courses for adults and the more diffused popular propaganda. But as yet only the towns enjoy these advantages to the full, and in the villages it is only the younger peasants who have been reached at all, and that chiefly in Central Russia, where there was no civil war. On the whole, the village tends to independence. It is helping itself through the revival of its primitive cottage industries and relying less and less on exchange with the towns.

In struggling, by inevitably harsh measures, against these tendencies, which spell collectively the ruin of urban civilization, the Communists necessarily make themselves unpopular. They may not provoke any formidable revolt, for even the Cossacks can always be subdued by artillery. Their most anxious military problem is the simmering brigandage in the Ukraine, and they have also reason to fear the assassination of their leaders. But they do, by this incessant battle to reverse the consequences latent in the agrarian revolution, over-strain their own powers of leadership and diminish by severity the receptivity both of peasants and workmen for their doctrines. There is, none the less, a perceptible weakening of the profit-making, gain-seeking mentality of capitalist civilization, which was always feeble in Russia. Some of the Intellectuals enjoy the new opportunities for disinterested and creative social service. A majority among Communist officials are moved by this motive. A few even of the peasants, as they group themselves for cultivation or for home industries in co-operative "artéls," are moving away from the old system of individualism and personal gain. Youth is eagerly embracing the new ideas, at all events in the towns, and there is in them an astonishing rush to enjoy the new opportunities of culture, especially on its æsthetic side.

The immediate future depends, as everyone realizes,

mainly on the restoration of peace and trade. If France, in pursuit of her implacable vendetta, is allowed to go on, year after year, hiring and equipping fresh enemies to attack Russia, she will inflict incalculable injury on its population and may bring its struggling civilization to ruin, but I do not believe that she will attain her end. The survival for many months of a Tsarist or semi-Tsarist regime, even if a military victory could restore it, is for me unthinkable. The peasants will not pay for the land they enjoy, while the moral inferiority of the self-indulgent Whites to the puritan Reds would not be altered by a momentary success. Even a stable Tsarism could not repay the French debt, however much it might recognize it. If, on the other hand, these subsidized attacks cease, then for the first time the Communists will have a fair chance of restoring industry. The organization of labour is still a problem, but the discipline is as good as it can be with half-fed workers. Industry will be demobilized, and what it produced for the Army can be used instead to buy food for the workers. With the ample and punctual rationing of the industrial workers their output will increase, and the difficulty of keeping them in the factories will diminish. The townsmen will be better fed, the countrymen better clothed, and the general increase of comfort will allay discontent. As the armies are disbanded, the return of the youthful population, which almost alone in Russia has will and ideas, must revive every department of production and education.

This year's failure of the crops, especially if it means a deficiency of seed, will certainly create an appalling problem. But since food will be short even in the villages of Central Russia, the workmen may be less reluctant to return to the towns and the peasants more willing to listen to good advice in the matter of cultivation and co-operation.

The revival of trade will have its dangers for Communism, as well as its advantages. To import tools of all kinds, from locomotives downwards, will be an unmixed gain. But if Moscow is tempted to ease its own difficulties by importing manufactured articles which might be made in Russia, it may itself succumb to the worst consequences of the agrarian revolution. If it allows industry to decay and relies on imports, it will lose in the end the none too numerous proletariat on which its rule is based. The admission of the capitalistic concession-holder will make a grave breach in Communist theory, and may also create new rallying-points for the opposition, more dangerous than the armed camps of the Whites. The hope of any really big reorganization of production in Russia depends on schemes which as yet the Communists have lacked the means to develop. They have plans for transferring industries to districts nearer to the raw materials and the coal. They have other schemes for specializing agricultural production in accordance with climate and soil, which, of course, presuppose a perfected transport system. Above all, there is Lenin's vision, which he has begun on a small scale to realize, of the complete electrification, within ten years, of Russian agriculture, industry and railways, organized, in thirty districts, with water-power, coal, oil, shale or peat as its bases. Peat is a poor fuel, and the distances are immense. I am not capable of judging the technical promise of this scheme, but it will soon be tested in action, for three of the central power stations are under construction. Its political attraction is clearly that it would, by a sort of instantaneous magic, break down the individualist agriculture and the individualist mentality of the Russian peasant. Cultivation by electrically driven machinery would mean the swift end of the primitive two-field holding, and the universal adoption of the big co-operative or communal farm. On this scheme, or on more modest variants of it, hangs the future of the Revolution. The introduction even of horse-drawn machinery, if there were enough of it, would have the same social effect. But Russia cannot be a Socialist Commonwealth while the mass of her population lives by individualistic peasant husbandry. The agrarian revolution has yet to be transformed into the Communist revolution. The abler leaders understand the problem clearly, and their schemes seem well fitted to solve it.

On the political as on the economic side the future of the Revolution depends no less clearly on internal and external peace. It will go to ruin, intellectually and morally, unless freedom of discussion and a reasonable licence for loyal political activities are soon introduced. No sane Government would allow full scope for agitation against itself by political adversaries during civil war, and so long as the atmosphere of civil war prevails the dictatorship will continue. There are grave faults on both sides. The Social Revolutionaries assisted Koltchák, and even the lesson of that experience did not prevent some of them from transferring their support to Deníkin and Wrangel. They retain, moreover, their old habit of political assassination, cultivated during Tsarist days. The Mensheviks have been much wiser, and incomparably more loyal to their own ideal of moderate Socialism, but even they confine themselves to protests, complaints and negative criticism. With peace and time the dictatorship may grow milder. It has achieved its negative purpose by destroying the capitalist system. In the task of building up, there is no longer a valid reason for refusing the co-operation of every group which will work loyally and positively for the future of the Socialist State. I doubt, however, whether the Communist party is likely to surrender voluntarily even the least of the outposts by which it maintains its monopoly of power. It is true to say of it that its mind has been formed by a quasi-religious fanaticism. The astonishing fact is, however, that with this doctrinaire starting-point it has none the less shown itself, under Lenin's leadership, so adaptable that its Russian critics in the other Socialist parties scoff at its compromises. The new system of one-man management in industry, the high rewards paid to specialists and the discrimination in wages between the more and less indispensable kinds of labour, based in reality on demand, to say nothing of the big concessions offered to foreigners, are all of them expedients which show how little rigidity there is in Lenin's application of his doctrines. The Communist party will not be easily displaced, nor do I see a party fit to displace it. On the other hand, its present discipline can hardly preserve its unity for ever, for there are sharply divergent tendencies within it. In the long run, the rapid progress in education in Russia is the guarantee that the form of representative government will become a reality, as the masses gain in knowledge and experience.

There are signs that the Communist party is itself alarmed by the growth of what it calls " bureaucracy."

It perceives the decadence of the Soviet system. Lenin has dwelt on this in a recent speech, and the pressure from within the Communist party towards genuine popular government is already powerful. But there is no effective remedy save freedom. One may well be hypercritical, however, in this matter. Has any representative system ever worked well in war-time ? But I confess to a doubt whether the traditional Western theory of liberty was really designed for a period of open conflict between two fundamentally opposed conceptions of society. The Liberal tradition was based on *laisser-faire*. If it is generally accepted that the State should never attempt any large interference in economic life, and never engage in any big effort of social construction, it is easy to maintain all the liberties of debate. For, after all, nothing fundamental can ever come up for discussion. There are signs that our own conception of liberty may not survive a sharpened class struggle. In the United States one State Legislature already excludes elected Socialist members. In England we are sending men to prison with hard labour for importing Communist literature. It is probable that the Capitalistic State will forbid Socialist propaganda so soon as it becomes a serious menace. Can one marvel if the Socialist State in its turn represses counter-revolutionary propaganda ? Liberty will be possible when the risk of forcible counter-revolution is over. A return to anything like the Western democratic form is, however, highly improbable. The political Soviets may possibly recover their pristine vigour. But it is more likely that the trade unions, which are in reality productive guilds, may be the most important governing bodies of the future, and that their elected councils may become the most effective instruments of representation.

*   *   *   *   *

I am closing these chapters without an attempt to estimate the general value of the Communist system as one may see it in Russia. Its form is too little fixed, its realization as yet too sketchy, for such a valuation. To judge Communism by its actual achievements in Russia, with an illiterate and primitive population as its human material, and the wreckage of war, civil war and blockade for its scene, is what no rational man would do unless he were heated by passion or fear. One might as well judge Capitalism by the misery of Poland or the depression of Esthonia. I will, however, attempt to record the personal impression which these two months in Russia made upon me.

One saw, indeed, in Communist Russia little that recalled the innocent and childlike paradise of William Morris and his comrades of dreamland. It is true that men were no longer elbowing each other in the competitive struggle. They were, however, running about with much anxiety to find food. Yet even when one allows for the scarcity of food and clothing, the mere material gain to millions of Russians is enormous. If for a moment I doubt that, I recall Tolstoy's pictures of the industrial system as he saw it in Moscow. You could not find to-day a group even faintly resembling that gang of railway goods porters who worked habitually for thirty-six hours on end and slept in a Black Hole that would have disgraced an eighteenth-century prison. Or take his picture of the silk weavers. Every detail is changed—the long hours, the neglect of the sick, the drunkenness, the abandoned children. No foreign student of this Revolution can possibly do it justice, for we cannot picture with sufficient vividness the oppressions which it has ended. Nor is the idyllic aspect wholly absent. Even William Morris, if he had heard the choir in Vladímir, watched the children in their camps and playing-fields, seen their drawings of fairy-tales and stood beside the village carpenters at work on their new models of handicraft, would have recognized some of the elements of his dream. I recall the prediction which formed itself in my mind as I saw the educational work of the Revolution. In ten years, I thought, if this nation enjoys peace, it will have made of its younger generation by far the happiest, by far the most cultivated nation of Europe. For as yet Europe has no cultivated nation, but only a number of relatively cultivated privileged classes. Nor need the knowledge that the backward peasantry remains outside the scope of these influences lead to a pessimistic conclusion. Nothing is required to bring the peasants into one form or another of collective and scientific husbandry but an ample supply of agricultural machines. Once these are available, the stupidest peasant must needs prefer them to his own laborious and unfruitful methods. That he understands to-day nothing either of the ideal or of the economic teaching of Socialism matters little. The intellectualist Liberal tradition builds too much on teaching, conviction and the workings of the self-moved mind. It is environment that makes the individualist or the Socialist. A man who works for the market on his own strip of land will be an individualist. A man will be a Socialist who works for a society which takes his superfluous products and gives him other goods in exchange, who works, moreover, in a team, dependent on his fellows. The power of Lenin as a statesman lies in this, that he understands the possibility of transforming men's minds by changing their outward conditions. With the machines he can recruit his teams ; from his teams he can make Communists. Many years, to be sure, will pass if Russia must first make her own machines. But can the world afford to wait ? Give him his machines and his locomotives, and after two or three harvests Russia might far surpass her pre-war export. By the mere substitution of a rational rotation of crops for her two or three field system, she would add over one-third to her effective acreage, besides increasing the return. If there were among the Allies even one man with the imagination of a statesman, the half-employed metal industry of Germany and Austria (not to mention our own) would be aided, if necessary with credits, to make machines for the half-tilled fields of Russia. The exchange of tools against grain would suffice to restore the civilization of Europe.[1]

[1] While I believe firmly in the great potentialities of Russia, it would be a mistake to exaggerate the immediate prospects for export. Russia must begin by importing machinery and tools of all kinds, from locomotives and motor-ploughs to scythes and saws. Her plan is to obtain these things on credit, by depositing a sufficient sum in gold in Western banks to cover her purchases. She proposes to pay, somewhat later, in exports. She has, of course, unlimited timber, but she cannot cut it or transport it, if war requires her again to mobilize the workers. She has an immediately available surplus of flax, and might increase her production if the peasants were sure of receiving payment in goods. Copper she might export, if war did not oblige her to retain it for munitions. There may be hoarded stocks of grain, though whether in good condition is doubtful ; but even these will

The dictatorship has endowed the Communist party with powers, which are in the abstract absolute, to drive through every obstacle for the attainment of its purposes. One can hardly exaggerate the gain from the abolition of interested obstruction to the social aims of a society. When the resolve is taken to raise the standard and increase the cost of education, there are no employing interests to be considered, none of that opposition, half mute, half vocal, from capitalists large and small, who in England will always scheme to thwart the larger purposes of a Minister of Education, partly because they desire the direct gains to be got from exploiting the labour of the young, and partly because they object to the enlightenment of the workers. The only obstacles to be met in Russia are poverty, the lack of teachers and the inertia of the people, and even these can be largely overcome when, at the first signal from the centre, a zealous and disciplined party instantly starts to create by " agitation " an atmosphere favourable to the prompt realization of a decree. That is where the new dictatorship differs from the old Autocracy. A Tsar commanded and left the execution of his orders to passive obedience. The Communists back every decree, whether it relates to education or health or industry, by an active educational campaign. The ease with which material improvements can be carried through, given the labour and the tools, seemed almost laughable.

be available only when Russian or foreign industry provides goods to exchange for them. With the reorganization of Russian agriculture there should again be a surplus for export much greater than that of Tsarist days. But it will be available only after several harvests, and only then if much machinery is first imported.

Does a factory want a narrow-gauge railway ? **It** has only to build it.   There are no private interests to be squared ; no landowners to be compensated ; no lawyers to be fee'd ; no Bill to be carried through a dilatory Legislature.   A dictatorship armed with such powers, and backed by such helpers, may dream without absurdity of raising the whole mental and material level of a people's life by one intense, heroic effort.

One must not, of course, confuse the abstract power of doing anything with the real power to achieve.   The assault on Russian inertia is terrific, but in the end the mere lethargy of the mass may wear down the energy of the builders.   Their rashness may in the end undo them.   For they are not content to limit their attack.   They alarm parental instincts ; they challenge the Church ; they ignore many a fixed tendency of Russian and even of human nature. They seem to revel in making difficulties for themselves and arousing opposition.   Again, it is obvious that their success depends entirely on raising the productivity of Russia, both in agriculture and in industry, and this they must achieve without the leverage of private gain.   That is the speculative element in all their work.   It is, like every revolution, a gamble with the unknown capacities of human nature for adaptation.   My own belief is that they will succeed, if they get peace.   I base my faith upon the pride which multitudes of young men and women, who did not seem exceptional, were taking in the mere contemplation of useful work well done.   I think of a corps of engineers at work on a bridge, whose foreman paused for a moment in his work to tell me how many bridges they had built in the year, solidly and in " record " time, or of the communal farm which displayed the results of one year's cultivation of hitherto untilled sand. That some will respond, when private profit and class exploitation is abolished, to the call of social service is proved already. The fate of the Revolution depends on the answer of experience to the question whether, with time and education, many will do so. It is too soon to answer certainly, but there is ground for a reasoned hope. One need assume no moral miracle. It is enough that some, who will supply the direction and the driving force, will put forth their utmost endeavour from pure zeal or from the love of distinction. The mass will work, as it does under any system, for food and clothes and the means of pleasure.

* * * * *

While waiting one afternoon in the Commissariat of Foreign Affairs in Moscow, I turned the pages of an American Sunday paper which was lying on the table. No experience which I had yet had in Russia had brought a shock of surprise so vivid. I had forgotten the spirit of the civilization which I had left behind me. The poverty, the simplicity, the strenuousness of this Russian life had come to seem natural and familiar. The almost insolent opulence of this newspaper startled me. I had got used to the slight Russian journals, badly printed on cheap paper. This thing reeked of wealth. The innumerable illustrations, produced by a costly process, were an amazement. I turned the pages like a pioneer breaking into a new world. On the whole, this world repelled me. Page after page described and illustrated one luxury after another. Costly clothes were offered to allure you, and half-dressed figures exhibited to display them. Here were cosmetics, there jewels, and again devices for curling the hair. The news pictures seemed to be a continuation of the advertisements. Here was a smiling lady, the daughter of a wealthy house, who had won a championship in rowing. Here was another, the wife of a millionaire, pretty, well formed, well dressed, whose speciality was horses. Next came a group of athletes from an expensive college, handsome, well built and obviously overfed. Turn the pages, and what else was there ? Actresses and actors and more sportsmen and sportswomen. I glanced at the letterpress. It was all of a piece. The same civilization had produced the advertisements, the photographs and the articles. The entire paper was devoted to celebrating the idle but pleasurable life of persons whose distinction lay in their wealth. Of art (save that of the commercial theatre), of science or even of religion there was no mention. What did this society live for ? What idea sustained it ? For what purpose did it exist on the earth ? If I had known nothing of it, if I had been a scholar examining this document, as one examines a Greek manuscript found in Egypt, I must have said : This society exists to fawn upon wealth, and its main ambition is to flaunt the jewels, the clothes and the idleness which only wealth can buy. As I laid down the paper and went out into the fresh air, there came into my memory that monumental phrase of Herbert Spencer's in which he admiringly defines the principle of a competitive capitalist society as " the beneficent private war, which makes one man strive to climb over the shoulders of another man." Here were the climbers.

I felt somehow at home again when I found myself

outside in the gardens of the Opera Square. The sun was shining and the flowers—homely stocks and roses—were gay without profusion. Everyone was plainly dressed, but the young girls in their simple cotton frocks looked healthy and happy. A mother went by on the arm of a Red soldier, a tall and well-built man, gaunt and bronzed, with something indefinably purposeful in his strength. On the benches groups were seated, reading books or talking. I heard fragments of conversation. One group was discussing recent poetry and another the Polish War. None of them challenged attention, for none were wearing new or showy clothes, but among them there were some thoughtful and some beautiful faces. An old man strolled past, playing skilfully and with an alluring and childlike joy upon a clarinet, and everyone thrust a gift into the bulging pockets of his coat. An old woman stopped me to ask the way, and she seemed to give me the clue to the homely simplicity of this scene, as she addressed me with the word now usual in Russia, " Comrade."

Then, from a side street, came the sound of singing, and a procession swung into view, advancing rapidly. They carried a banner with the familiar motto, " Workers of all lands unite," and their song was the most popular and arresting of the Red Army's marching choruses. There were old and young among them, but chiefly young, and many were women. I remembered that it was Saturday afternoon. They were Communists evidently going to a " Saturdaying "—a half day of voluntary physical work done without payment, to carry help where help is needed. I followed them, and presently came on a group just starting operations. They broke step, ran to their places and took off their coats without the loss of a moment. The girls even took off their shoes and stockings, and presently were carrying bricks with rapidity and method. I stood and watched them, alternately thinking of that purposeless society of the American pictures and of this scene of hard work and social zeal before me. Half amused, half annoyed, a working woman remarked, as she brushed past me, " It's easily seen that you're a *bourjóee* [Russian pronunciation of bourgeois]. You look on while others work."

*   *   *   *   *

In spite of the physical misery, most of it due to war, in spite of much intolerance and much callousness, in spite even of the suppression of political liberty, I had the sense that I was watching a gigantic effort of creation. The struggle of this shaping and creative Communist ideal to master its recalcitrant material, was to me all the more impressive because I felt beneath it the presence of the other tendency, the wrecking, destructive mutiny of a Slav peasantry. The positive work of the Revolution, whether one saw it in the factory, the farm or the school, is an epic triumph, not only over foreign enemies and the armed reaction, but also over these darker forces in the untaught Russian soul. Squalor there may be, and poverty, and yet I think that this Revolution will live to vindicate itself in history as the greatest effort of the constructive human will since the French made an end of feudalism. Liberal democracy is not in itself a creative or architectural principle. What it does, is to keep the arena in which contemporary forces struggle for opportunity. Among these forces our own civilization has thrown up as yet none which can compare in efficacy with the egoistic motive of private gain. In Russia a social principle has, by violence, indeed, and a contemptuous disregard of democracy, made for itself an opportunity, which it uses with masterful will. It has broken the power of wealth to control men's lives. It is acting, even when it coerces them, for the sole good of the masses. It is making, even if it be destined to overthrow, a superb monument to the human will. To evolve a victorious army from an invertebrate rabble, to rouse a lazy and apathetic nation, amid poverty and suffering, to a task which demanded an almost insane courage, to conceive the daring ambition of making a ruling caste out of young, unschooled workmen, was in itself an act of audacity to which time has no parallel. Beyond the bravery of this struggle there lies a much vaster design—to change the entire economic structure of this half-continent, and with it the mind of a race. There are those who believe that initiative, ambition and the creative will are evolved only by the hope of personal gain. Here is initiative, here is the will to reshape and create, on a scale to which all our civilization together offers no parallel.

Its actual achievement will be hampered by the original poverty and intellectual immaturity of Russia ; it may be frustrated by the criminal enmity of Western politicians. I will sum up what I have seen of its tendency in one sentence. It is, in a land where a feeble and dilatory civilization had touched as yet only a minute minority of a gifted population, a great and heroic attempt to shorten the dragging march of time, to bring culture to a whole nation, and to make a co-operative society where a predatory despotism, in the act of suicide, had prepared the general ruin.